Education for Action

Undergraduate and Graduate Programs that Focus on Social Change

Expanded, third edition

edited by Sean Brooks
and Alison Knowles

A Food First Book © 1995
The Institute for Food and Development Policy
Oakland, California

ACKNOWLEDGMENTS

This expanded edition was compiled by a team of Food First research interns, coordinated by Sean Brooks and Alison Knowles. Also contributing to the project were: Shanna Langdon, Gavin Post, Li Kheng Poh, and Abikök Riak.

Food First staff members provided editorial consultation: Marilyn Borchardt, John Gershman, Kathleen McClung, and Peter Rosset.

Thanks to Theo Crawford for proofreading services, Lory Poulson for cover design, and Harvest Graphics for design, typesetting, and indexing assistance.

Library of Congress Cataloging-in-Publication Data

Education for action : undergraduate and graduate programs that focus
    on social change / edited by Sean Brooks and Alison Knowles. —
    Expanded, 3rd ed.
        p.   cm.
    Includes index.
    ISBN 0-935028-64-1
    1. Social sciences — Study and teaching (Higher) — Directories.
2. Social change — Study and teaching (Higher) — Directories.
I. Brooks, Sean. II. Knowles, Alison. III. Institute for Food and
Development Policy (Oakland, Calif.)
H62.E328   1995
300'.71' 173 — dc20   95-24741
                                                                CIP

Printed in USA
10 9 8 7 6 5 4 3 2 1
To order additional copies, please write or call our distributor:
Subterranean Company
Box 160, 265 South Fifth Street
Monroe, OR   97456
800-274-7826

TABLE OF CONTENTS

Introduction iv

Programs:

    Agriculture 1

    Anthropology 7

    Area Studies 15
        Africa
        Latin America
        Asia

    Development/International Relations 25

    Economics 31

    Education 39

    Environment 45

    Ethnic Studies 49

    Geography 57

    History 63

    Human Rights 65

    Law 67

    Peace Studies 73

    Political Science 87

    Public Health/Nutrition 89

    Sociology 97

    Urban Planning 107

    Women's Studies 113

Index 119

INTRODUCTION

First published in 1987, *Education for Action* filled a void for students researching socially responsible graduate programs. Eight years later, the third edition remains the only comprehensive guide of its kind offering graduate and undergraduate programs focusing on social change.

Food First's mission is to chronicle and affirm the struggle for the basic human right of freedom from hunger and from the injustices that cause hunger. This is social change we support. Furthermore, we believe that education and action are the fundamental components of social change, and we at Food First believe the most effective, truly transformative curricula integrate both education and action.

Given these guiding principles, this latest edition of *Education for Action* is larger and more comprehensive than ever. It includes:

• undergraduate programs

• new graduate programs

• expanded format with program description, course highlights, key faculty, and contact information

• completely new sections featuring Area Studies, Education, Environment, Geography, and Human Rights

The courses and faculty we have highlighted are not always representative of the whole program and should not be construed as such. There are also many interesting choices to be made within a program, such as designing a major, double majoring, or stopping out for interesting internships, work, or overseas programs.

As a guide for students and guidance counselors, *Education for Action* represents the recommendations of Food First and its academic collaborators and is not an exhaustive list of progressive programs. We hope that successive editions will continue to grow and draw from a larger and increasingly diverse pool of programs focusing on social change. We also hope readers of this book continue the struggle for world peace and an equitable distribution of resources.

What follow are our recommendations and our wish for your success in school, career, and life. We are glad that you are joining us in seeking social change through education and action. Maintain a critical mind and compassionate heart, and remember that all programs have both strengths and weaknesses, advantages and disadvantages. What you put in contributes to what you get out of any program.

Agriculture

Cornell University

Cornell University
Section of Ecology and Systematics
Field of Ecology and Evolutionary Biology
Corson Hall
Ithaca, NY 14853-2701

Ecology and Systematics

Degrees: B.S., M.A., Ph.D.

Phone	607/255-4522
Fax	607/255-8088
E-mail	eeb_grad_req@cornell.edu

Under the Division of Biological Sciences, the Section of Ecology and Systematics has 18 full-time faculty and nine joint or adjunct appointments from other sections or departments. The section is known for its scholarship in ecology and vertebrate biology, and has recently added faculty focusing on evolutionary biology. Graduate students are admitted to Cornell University through graduate fields rather than through departments or sections. All members of the faculty in the Section of Ecology and Systematics are members of the Field of Ecology and Evolutionary Biology, and some are members of other fields as well. *Undergraduate Course Highlights: Ecology and the Environment; Population and Evolutionary Ecology; Food, Agriculture, and Society; Ecology of Agricultural Systems.*

✦ Key Faculty

Alison Power: Sustainable agriculture and biological pest control in the U.S. and Latin America; member of the fields of Ecology and Evolutionary Biology, Entomology, International Agriculture, Conservation and Sustainable Development, and the Latin American Studies Program.
Admissions Information: Graduate Faculty Representative; (Address as above).

Hampshire College

Hampshire College
Agricultural Studies (& Other Programs)
School of Natural Science
Amherst, MA 01002

Agricultural Studies

Degree: B.A.

Phone	413/582-5486
Fax	413/582-5448
E-mail	bschultz@ hamp.hampshire.edu

Hampshire College is a fully accredited alternative college that does not use grades or credits but emphasizes education based on independent and group projects. Social justice is an essential component of the college, along with other programs such as Public Service and Social Change, Third World Studies, and more. The college collaborates with other institutions in promoting sustainable food systems and on many other projects in New England and around the world.

The School of Natural Science has three focus areas: biomedical science, agricultural studies, and environmental science/alternative technology. The program includes the Hampshire College Farm Center and the Bioshelter, and connects issues in agriculture to the broader political, historical, and social framework in which agriculture takes place in this country and the Third World. *Course Highlights: Pesticide Alternatives; World Food Crisis; Third World Health; Sustainable Agriculture.*

✦ *Key Faculty*

Brian Schultz: Ecology; agriculture; statistics; social change; U.S.; Central America.
Admissions Information: Director of Admissions; Hampshire College; Amherst, MA 01002; Phone 413/582-5471.

University of California, Berkeley

Biological Control

College of Natural Resources
Department of Environmental Science,
    Policy, and Management
145 Mulford Hall #3114
University of California
Berkeley, CA 94720-3114

Degrees: M.A., Ph.D.

Phone   510/642-6410
Fax   510/643-5438
E-mail espmgradproginfo@
        nature.berkeley.edu

The Laboratory of Biological Control is one of the facilities run by the recently consolidated Department of Environmental Science, Policy, and Management. The department offers degrees in Entomology, Plant Pathology, Soil Science, Wildland Resource Science, as well as a Master of Forestry. The department hopes to have an integrated graduate program Fall of 1996. *Course Highlights: Agriculture Ecology; Biological Control of Pests; Field Entomology.*

✦ *Key Faculty*

Miguel Altieri: Agroecology of crop and pest management in California; small farm development in Latin America.
Admissions Information: (Address as above).

University of California, Santa Cruz

Agroecology

Agroecology Program
Department of Environmental Studies
University of California
Santa Cruz, CA 95064

Degrees: B.S. (Envir. Studies), M.A.,
Ph.D.
Phone 408/459-4140
Fax 408/459-2799

The University of California, Santa Cruz provides a combined Ph.D./M.A. program through Environmental Studies that focuses on the interdisciplinary aspects of sustainable agriculture. Topics include: on-farm transitions to sustainable practices, public policy to support sustainability, alternative pest control measures, soil management, and social issues in sustainability. Undergraduate students can participate in the Agroecology Program by pursuing the Agroecology and Sustainable Agriculture Area of Concentration within the Environmental Studies major. The program manages two facilities: an organic 4-acre garden and 25-acre farm. *Course Highlights: Agroecology and Sustainable Agriculture; Integrated Pest Management; Sustainable Soil Management; Political Economy of Sustainable Agriculture in Latin America.*

✦ *Key Faculty*

Steve Gliessman: Director, Agroecology Program; environmental and biological issues related to Third World development; alternative agriculture; converting to sustainable agriculture management.
Admissions Information: Division of Graduate Studies; Board of Environmental Studies; 399 Applied Sciences Building; University of California; Santa Cruz, CA 95064; Phone 408/459-3718.

University of Maine

Sustainable Agriculture

University of Maine
Sustainable Agriculture Program
Department of Applied Ecology and
        Environmental Sciences
5722 Deering Hall
Orono, ME 04469-5722

Degrees: B.S., M.A., Ph.D.

Phone 207/581-2926
Fax 207/581-2999

The program is rooted in the natural sciences and economics, with special emphasis on soil, crop, and pest ecology and management. Research activities are conducted at the university's Rogers and Aroostook farms as well as on commercial farms. Degree options for the M.A. include: bio-resource engineering; botany and plant pathology; ecology and environmental sciences; entomology; plant, soil and environmental sciences; resource economics and policy; and resource utilization. Ph.D.s are offered in biological sciences, ecology and environmental sciences, plant science, or an individualized program. *Course Highlights: Agricultural Ecology; Pesticides and the Environment; Pest-Plant Interactions.*

✦ Key Faculty

Matt Liebman: Sustainable agriculture; weed ecology.
Admissions Information: (Address as above).

University of Michigan

Biology

University of Michigan
Department of Biology
Natural Science Building
Ann Arbor, MI 48109

Degrees: M.A., Ph.D.

Phone   313/764-1443
Fax   313/747-0884

Ecology, Evolution, and Organismal Biology covers topics such as behavior, biogeochemistry, biogeography, life history models, selection, speciation, species interactions, and phylogenetics. Environmental Biology studies biological productivity, nutrient cycles, and trophic dynamics of aquatic and terrestrial ecosystems, environmental physiology, biogeochemistry, and mechanisms of biological interaction between environment and organism at organismic, cellular, molecular, and behavioral levels. *Course Highlights: Tropical Biology: An Ecological Approach; Dynamic Systems in Population and Community Ecology; Ecology of Agroecosystems; The Dynamics of Neotropical Rainforests.*

✦ Key Faculty

John Vandermeer: Tropical ecology: tropical rainforest dynamics, tropical agroecology, and tropical conservation; Costa Rica; Nicaragua.
Admissions Information: Graduate Coordinator; Department of Biology; Natural Science Building; Ann Arbor, MI 48109-1048; Phone 313/764-1443.

University of Minnesota

University of Minnesota
Department of Entomology
219 Hodson Hall
1980 Folwell Avenue
St. Paul, MN 55108

Entomology

Degrees: Ph.D. Entomology, Ph.D.
Conservation Biology, M.S. Sustainable
Agriculture (likely spring 1995)
Phone   612/624-3636
Fax   612/625-5299
E-mail   holze001@
maroon.tc.umn.edu

Specializations in entomology include behavior, ecology, molecular genetics, microbiology, neurobiology, physiology, population dynamics, systematics, and taxonomy. Applications involve agriculture, biological control, cell culture, host-plant resistance, insect-vector relations, integrated pest management, and modeling. *Course Highlights: Insect-Pest Management; Ecology of Agriculture; Biological Control of Insects.*

✦ *Key Faculty*

David Andow: Sustainable agriculture; conservation biology; insect population management; biotechnology; U.S.; Japan.
Admissions Information: (Address as above); Phone 612/625-5299; Fax 612/625-5299.

OTHER PROGRAMS

Department of Agricultural and
      Resource Economics
University of California
Berkeley, CA 94720
✦ *Key Faculty:* **Alain de Janvry**

Degree: Ph.D.
Phone   510/642-3345
Fax   510/643-8911

Anthropology

American University

Anthropology

American University
Department of Anthropology
4400 Massachusetts Avenue, NW
Washington, DC 20016-8003

Degrees: B.A., M.A.A., M.A., Ph.D.

Phone   202/885-1830
Fax   202/885-1837

Department's geographical foci include Africa, the Americas, and South Asia. Concentrations include complex societies, urban anthropology, cultural resource management, bilingual education, international development, culture change, and ethnicity, as well as the transformation of rural society. In addition to the B.A., M.A. and the Ph.D. degrees, the department offers an M.A. in applied anthropology. *Course Highlights: Food and Culture; Refugees: Survival, Adaptation & Transformation; Cultural Construction of Gender.*

✦ *Key Faculty*

Brett Williams: Poverty (coping strategies and organizing for social change); racism; credit and debt.
Admissions Information: Office of Graduate Affairs and Admissions; The American University; 4400 Massachusetts Avenue, NW; Washington, DC 20016-8111; Phone 202/885-1098.

Columbia University

Anthropology

Columbia University
Department of Anthropology
New York, NY 10027

Degrees: M.A., Ph.D.
Phone   212/854-4552
Fax   212/854-7347

The doctoral program prepares students for teaching at the university level, for museum and archaeological work, and for independent research and writing. Fields of study include sociocultural anthropology (economic, aesthetic, legal, medical, urban), archaeology, and biological anthropology. Faculty geographical strengths include Africa, East Asia, Europe, Latin America, the Middle East, and the U.S. *Course Highlights: Latin American Communities; Life in Rural South Asia; Food and Society; African Peoples in the World System; Magic of the State; Women in Development.*

✦ Key Faculty

Michael Taussig: Director of Graduate Studies; political economy; medical anthropology; colonialism; peasant societies; Latin America.
Admissions Information: Graduate School of Arts and Sciences; Office of Admissions and Financial Aid; 107 Low Memorial Library; Columbia University; New York, NY 10027; Phone 212/854-4552.

New School for Social Research

Anthropology

New School for Social Research
Department of Anthropology
65 Fifth Avenue
New York, NY 10003

Degrees: M.A., Ph.D.

Phone 212/229-5757
Fax 212/229-5757 (Same as phone)

The program focuses on the theoretical and methodological foundations of social and cultural anthropology in the areas of cultural theory, gender, anthropology, and history. *Course Highlights: Social History of Development in Africa; Theoretical Approaches to Race and Racism; Culture and Political Economy; Feminist Theory; International Perspectives; Land and Labor in Latin America.*

✦ Key Faculty

Rayna Rapp: Chair; political economy; women's studies; women and health.
Admissions Information: Graduate Faculty Admissions; New School for Social Research; 65 Fifth Avenue, Room 110; New York, NY 10003; Phone 800/523-5411.

San Francisco State University

Anthropology

San Francisco State University
Department of Anthropology
1600 Holloway Avenue
San Francisco, CA 94132

Degree: M.A.

Phone 415/338-2046
Fax 415/338-0530

The anthropology program at San Francisco State University covers three of the four primary sub fields of anthropology: archaeology, socio/cultural anthropology, and biological/physical anthropology.

Four of the Department's eight full-time faculty members are cultural anthropologists and have a special commitment to studying applied issues and to addressing the urgent social crises of the urban United States. The department also has expertise in China, Korea, and Central America. *Course Highlights: Seminar in Archaeological Problems; Physical Anthropology; Problems in Cultural Anthropology.*

✦ **Key Faculty**

Phillipe Bourgois: Political economy; cultural production theory; ethnicity; immigration and the work process; gender relations; inner city social marginalization; substance abuse; ethnographic methods; Latino/as in the United States; Central America.
James Quesada: Cultural anthropology; medical anthropology; psychological anthropology; migration and refugee studies; Central America.
Admissions Information: (Address as above).

Stanford University

Student Program Coordinator
Department of Anthropology
Stanford University
Stanford, CA 94305-2145

Anthropology

Degrees: M.A., Ph.D.

Phone   415/723-4641
Fax   415/725-0605

The Anthropology Department at Stanford is currently developing two programmatic foci: Comparative Cultural Studies and Human Biocultural Evolution. Comparative Cultural Studies concerns differences of race, class, national origin, gender, sexual orientation, and religion as shaped by history, migration, education, and other experiences through which people in contemporary societies define themselves in relation to others. Human Biocultural Evolution emphasizes biological and cultural aspects of human evolution, and their interaction, during the last few hundred thousand years. *Course Highlights: Culture and Power (Mesoamerica and Beyond); Seminar on African Law; Nationalism and Gender; Political Ecology.*

✦ **Key Faculty**

George Collier: Social anthropology; history; quantitative methods; Spain; Mesoamerica; Latin America.
Jane Collier: Cultural anthropology; anthropology of law; political anthropology; feminist theory; Mesoamerica; Southern Europe.

William Durham: Biological anthropology; ecological and evolutionary anthropology; demography; Mesoamerica.
Reynato Rosaldo: History; society; U.S. Latinos; islands of Southeast Asia, Latin America.
Admissions Information: Graduate Admissions Office; Stanford University; Stanford, CA 94305-3005; Phone 415/723-4291.

University of California, Berkeley

Anthropology

Department of Anthropology
232 Kroeber Hall
University of California
Berkeley, CA 94720

Degree: B.A., M.A. in folklore, Ph.D.

Phone 510/642-3391
Fax 510/643-8557

The Department of Anthropology offers training in social/cultural anthropology, archaeology, and biological anthropology. There is also a M.A. in folklore that draws on an interdisciplinary faculty. *Course Highlights: Social Inequality; Circumpolar Peoples; Mesoamerica (Maya Text and Image); Comparative Gender Systems.*

✦ Key Faculty

Gerald Berreman: Social/cultural anthropology; social inequality; interaction theory; research methods and ethics; urban society; small-scale societies; India; Himalayas; Arctic.
Laura Nader: Social anthropology; comparative ethnography of law and dispute resolution; conflict; controlling processes; comparative family organizations; anthropology of professional mind-sets; ethnology of the Middle East, Mexico, Latin America, and contemporary U.S.
Aihwa Ong: Cultural change; work; gender and sexuality; colonialism; immigrants; SE Asia; Pacific Rim.
Paul Rabinow: Cultural anthropology; social thought; modernity; France.
Nancy Scheper-Hughes: Medical anthropology; psychological anthropology; culture; madness and psychiatry; critical theory; gender; U.S. ethnic groups; Ireland; Western Europe; Brazil.
Admissions Information: (Address as above).

University of California, Davis

Anthropology

Department of Anthropology
University of California
Davis, CA 95616

Degrees: M.A., Ph.D.
Phone　916/752-0745
Fax　916/752-8885

The faculty provide instruction in all four of anthropology's subdisciplines: archaeology and biological, sociocultural, and linguistic anthropology. Each graduate student is admitted to a particular subdiscipline. Dr. Smith is associated with the UC Davis Hemispheric Initiative on the Americas, an interdisciplinary program that focuses on issues and problems common to the Americas, especially those concerning minority rights, nation-building, gender inequality, and mestizaje. *Course Highlights: Rural Transformation in Postcolonial Societies; Problems in Urban Anthropology; Gender, Identity, and Self.*

✦ *Key Faculty*

Carol Smith: Political economy; agrarian societies; race/class/gender ideologies in Central America; Mesoamerica.
Admissions Information: Graduate Studies; 252 Mrak Hall; University of California; Davis, CA 95616.

University of California, San Francisco

Medical Anthropology

University of California, San Francisco
Medical Anthropology Program
Department of Epidemiology and Biostatistics
School of Medicine
1350 Seventh Avenue, Room 317
San Francisco, CA 94143-0850

Degree:　Ph.D.

Phone　415/476-7234
Fax　415/476-6715

This is a joint program run by UCSF and the University of California at Berkeley. The program focuses on Third World health care delivery as well as U.S. health care programs and community health issues. Applications are accepted in odd-numbered years for admissions in even-numbered years. *Course Highlights: Stigmatized Health Conditions; Urban Anthropology; Seminar in Contemporary American Society.*

✦ **Key Faculty**

Joan Ablon: (Emerita-recalled to service); stigmatized health conditions; chronic illness; physical disability; dwarfism; genetic disorders; therapeutic self-help groups; social support systems.

Linda Mitteness: Interim Chair, Medical Anthropology Program; cultural construction of chronic illness; aging; culture of biomedicine; research methods; psychological anthropology; research ethics.

Admissions Information: Chair, Admissions Committee; (Address as above). Students contemplating entry via the Berkeley Campus should address inquiries to Administrative Assistant; Medical Anthropology Program; Department of Anthropology; University of California; Berkeley, CA 94720.

University of California, Santa Barbara

Anthropology

Department of Anthropology
University of California
Santa Barbara, CA 93106

Degrees: B.A., M.A., Ph.D.
Phone   805/893-2257
Fax   805/893-8707

The Anthropology Department offers majors in two undergraduate emphasis areas, one in physical anthropology, the other in cultural anthropology which includes both ethnology and archaeology. The physical anthropology major is highly structured and incorporates course requirements in biology and zoology. The cultural anthropology major is designed for both structure and flexibility. It allows a student to choose a variety of courses under the five classifications: theory and method; topics in ethnology and archaeology; development, ecology, and social change; ethnography and culture history; and physical anthropology. *Undergraduate Course Highlights: Culture and the Individual; Magic, Religion, and Witchcraft; People, Poverty, and Environment in Central America; Understanding Africa.*

There are three specializations in the M.A. and Ph.D. programs: archaeology, ethnology, and biological anthropology; additional specializations are possible within each of these fields. *Graduate Course Highlights: War and Coalitional Aggression; Peasants and Industrialization; Anthropology of World System; Anthropology of Development; Anthropology of Mass Media and Popular Culture.*

✦ *Key Faculty*

Susan Stonich: Effects of economic development on human societies and the natural environment in Central America.
Admissions Information: (Address as above).

OTHER PROGRAMS

City University of New York
Graduate Center
Department of Anthropology
✦ *Key Faculty:* **Marc Edelman**

University of Kentucky
Department of Anthropology
211 Lafferty Hall
Lexington, KY 40506-0024
✦ *Key Faculty:* **John van Willigen**

Degrees: M.A., Ph.D.
Phone   606/257-2710
Fax   606/258-1959

University of Texas-Austin
Department of Anthropology
✦ *Key Faculty:* **Edmond Gordon, Charles Hale**

Area Studies-Africa

Howard University

African Studies

Department of African Studies
Howard University
2400 6th Street, NW
Washington, DC 20059

Degrees: B.A., M.A., Ph.D.

Phone   202/806-7115

The Department of African Studies has a long history at Howard University. In 1953, the Department offered a Master's degree in African Studies, and in 1969 added a Ph.D. program, the first university to offer a Ph.D. in African Studies. The Department seeks to provide students with an objective view of the present situation in Africa and its role in the changing world. Students explore Africa's economic, social, and political problems. Interdisciplinary in nature, the program offers classes from a variety of fields. *Course Highlights: African Cultural Formation and Identity; Public Policy and Development in Africa; Social Stratification in Contemporary Africa.*

✦ *Key Faculty*

Bob Edgar: Southern Africa, Botswana.
Admissions Information:
Office of Admissions and Student Recruitment; Graduate School of Arts and Sciences; Howard University; 4th and College Streets, NW; Washington, DC 20059.

University of California, Los Angeles

African Studies

James S. Coleman African Studies Center
10244 Bunche Hall
405 Hilgard Avenue
University of California
Los Angeles, CA 90024-1310

Degrees: Undergrad Certificate, M.A.

Phone   310/825-3686
Fax   310/206-2250

Founded in 1959, the African Studies Center was established to stimulate growing interest in the region and to develop outreach, academic, and research programs on Africa. The center is dedicated to educating undergraduate and graduate students as well as the community about African languages, culture and society, and research, encouraging dialogue from all sectors. The center offers over 70 undergraduate and graduate courses taught by UCLA's renowned

Africanist scholars. The Master of Arts in African Area Studies provides each student with interdisciplinary breadth and depth as well as expertise in a chosen area of concentration. Demonstrated language ability is also necessary for the M.A. *Course Highlights: Swahili; Zulu; Hausa; Wolof; Government and Politics in Sub-Saharan Africa; Film and Social Change; African Women's History.*

✦ *Key Faculty*

Teshome Gabriel: African film.
Admissions Information: (Address as above); Phone 310/825-2944.

University of Wisconsin-Madison

African Studies

African Studies Program
University of Wisconsin-Madison
1454 Van Hise Hall
1220 Linden Drive
Madison, WI 53706

Degrees: Undergrad & Grad Certificate,
    Ph.D. Minor

Phone   608/262-2380
Fax   608/265-5851

The African Studies program includes a broad range of disciplines in which students at the graduate and undergraduate level may develop their study of Africa. The program offers courses from 25 departments in four colleges or schools, but does not grant degrees. Graduate students interested in Africa may earn a Ph.D. minor in African Studies or a certificate in African Studies. Undergraduates may choose a concentration in African Studies. Students emphasize African Studies in the context of their major or they may receive a B.A. in African Languages and Literature. Undergraduates also have the option of designing their own major in African Studies. The African Studies program encourages study abroad and offers programs in Tanzania, Senegal, Morocco, and Egypt. *Course Highlights: The African Autobiography; History of Black Nationalism: A Comparative Perspective; Peoples and Cultures of Africa.*

✦ *Key Faculty*

Gay Seidman: Third World labor movements; South Africa; Brazil.
Graduate Admissions Information: Graduate Admissions; Graduate School; 225 Bascom Hall; Madison, WI 53706-1380.
Undergraduate Admissions Information: Undergraduate Admissions; 140 Peterson Office Building; University of Wisconsin-Madison; Madison, WI 53706.

Other Africanists and Programs

Northern Arizona University
Department of Political Science
PO Box 15036
Flagstaff, AZ 86011
✦ *Key Faculty:* **Carol Thompson**

Phone   520/523-3163

City College
City University of New York (CUNY)
Department of History
138 Convent Avenue
New York, NY 10031
✦ *Key Faculty:* **David Johnson**

Degrees: B.A., M.A.
Phone   212/650-7137

Clark University
Program for International Development
    and Social Change
950 Main Street
Worcester, MA 01610-1477
✦ *Key Faculty:* **Ann Seidman**

Degree: M.A.
Phone   508/793-7201

Africana Studies & Research Center
Cornell University
310 Triphammer Road
Ithaca, NY 14850-2599

Degree: Undergrad Certificate, M.A.
Phone   607/255-4625

Michigan State University-East Lansing
Department of Anthropology
East Lansing, MI 48824
✦ *Key Faculty:* **William Derman**

Phone   517/353-2950

Rutgers University
Department of Urban Planning
PO Box 5078
New Brunswick, NJ 08903-5078
✦ *Key Faculty:* **Meredeth Turshen**

Degrees: M.S., Ph.D.
Phone   908/932-3822

University of Georgia-Athens
History Department
University of Georgia
Athens, GA 30602

Degrees: A.B., M.A., Ph.D.
Phone   706/542-2053

✦ *Key Faculty:* **David Schoenbrun**

University of Illinois-Champaign Urbana
Department of Sociology
326 Lincoln Hall
702 S. Wright Street
Urbana, IL 61801

Degrees: B.A., Ph.D.
Phone   217/333-1950

✦ *Key Faculty:* **William G. Martin**

University of Minnesota-Minneapolis
Department of History
Room 614 Social Sciences Building
267 19th Avenue South
Minneapolis, MN 55455

Degrees: B.A., M.A., Ph.D.
Phone   612/624-2800

✦ *Key Faculty:* **Allen Isaacman**

University of North Carolina
Department of History
Hamilton Hall
Campus Box 3195
University of North Carolina-Chapel Hill
Chapel Hill, NC 27599-3195

Degrees: B.A., M.A., Ph.D.
Phone   919/962-2115

✦ *Key Faculty:* **David Newbury**

Area Studies-Latin America

Institute of Latin American Studies

Latin American Studies/Latin American Politics/ Environmental Issues in Latin American Literature and Culture

University of London
Institute of Latin American Studies
31 Tavistock Square
London WC1H 9HA

Degrees: M.A., M.Sc., Ph.D., M.Phil.

Phone   +44 171 387 5671
Fax   +44 171 388 5024

Established in 1965 under the auspices of the University of London, the Institute of Latin American Studies was created for the study of Latin America only. The specialized form of the degrees allows students to focus more deeply on their particular area of interest: literature, environmental issues, or politics. Students who do the M.A. in Area Studies are offered a wide range of courses taken from a variety of disciplines including politics, economics, environment, literature and culture, sociology, and anthropology. *Course Highlights: Indian and Peasant Politics, Introduction to Economics; Welfare and Poverty in the 20th Century; Perspectives on Gender in Spanish-American Literature.*

✦ Key Faculty

James Dunkerley: Politics and history; political thought; military institutions and ideology; radical movements and ideas; Central America; Bolivia; the Southern Cone.
Maxine Molyneux: Sociology/political sociology; gender; development; socialist/communist states; Central America; Southern Cone.
Admissions Information: The Postgraduate Administrator; (Address as above).

Stanford University

Latin American Studies

Stanford University
Center for Latin American Studies
Bolivar House, 582 Alvarado Row
Stanford, CA 94305-8545

Degree: M.A.

Phone   415/723-4444
Fax   415/723-9822

Stanford University has an excellent Center for Latin American Studies. *Course Highlights: Perspectives on Sustainable Development in Latin America; The United States and Central America; The Agrarian Origins of Underdevelopment in Latin America.*

✦ **Key Faculty**

Terry Karl: Director, Center for Latin American Studies; democratization and peace accords; comparative politics; political economy of development; Latin America.

Kathleen Morrison: Assoc. Director, Center for Latin American Studies; street children in Latin America.

Admissions Information:
Office of Graduate Admissions; Old Union Bldg., Rm. 138; Stanford University; Stanford, CA 94305-3005.

University of California, Berkeley

Latin American Studies

Center for Latin American Studies
2334 Bowditch Street #2312
University of California
Berkeley, CA 94720-2312

Degrees: B.A., M.A., Ph.D.

Phone   510/642-2088
Fax   510/642-3260

This program is interdisciplinary in nature. Faculty and courses are drawn from other departments including Sociology, Anthropology, Economics, Geography, Ethnic Studies, Political Science, and History.

✦ **Key Faculty**

Laura Enriquez: Development in Latin America; rural sociology; social policy; social movement; Nicaragua, Cuba.

Peter Evans: Development; comparative political economy; state and industrialism; Latin America.

Beatriz Manz: Political ecology of the Third World; peasantry and indigenous, migrant and refugee populations; ethnography in Guatemala; refugee population in Mexico; U.S.-Mexican border.

Admissions Information: (Address as above).

University of London

Economics with special reference to Latin America

University of London
Queen Mary and Westfield College
Economics
327 Mile End Road
London E1 4NS

Degree: M.Sc.

Phone   +44 171 975 5555
Fax   +44 171 975 5500

This program was created for economists whose specific area of interest is Latin America. It offers an economics degree, but provides students with a much more focused program than traditional economics. It is designed for those who wish to specialize within their Master's, and graduate with a deeper knowledge of this particular region.

✦ Key Faculty

Victor Bulmer-Thomas: Director, Institute for Latin American Studies; poverty and income distribution; regional integration, including NAFTA; economic relations with Europe; Central American economics.
Admissions Information: (Address as above).

University of Massachusetts, Amherst — Latin American Studies

University of Massachusetts, Amherst	Degrees: Undergrad and Grad
Latin American Studies Program	Certificate
Thompson Hall 934	Phone 413/545-0455
Amherst, MA 01003	Fax 413/545-2921

The university offers an undergraduate certificate in Latin American Studies, in support of a disciplinary major. It is now developing a graduate certificate in Latin American Studies to be earned in conjunction with any disciplinary Master's or Ph.D. degree. It is planned for the graduate certificate to be offered in conjunction with 13 departments and professional schools. The strongest graduate programs offering a concentration in Latin American Studies include Economics, Spanish and Portuguese, Communication, and Education.

✦ Key Faculty

Carmen Diana Deere: Latin American political economy; agricultural development in Latin America; women and development; Cuba; Central America; the Andes.
James Boyce: Political economy; agricultural development; environmental economics; Central America; South and Southeast Asia.
Henry Geddes-Gonzalez: Communication and social change in the Third World; international mass media; media, culture, and ethnicity.

University of Texas at Austin

Latin American Studies

University of Texas at Austin
Institute of Latin American Studies
Sid W. Richardson Hall, Unit 1
Austin, TX 78712-1284

Degrees: B.A., M.A., Ph.D.

Phone 512/471-5551
Fax   512/471-3090

The Master's degree at UT Austin is multidisciplinary in nature and comprises courses from the Departments of Anthropology, Economics, Folklore, Sociology, and Government, among others. Since the Latin American Studies program is a highly flexible one, students need to plan a cohesive course of study to focus their interests. *Course Highlights: Political Development and Modernization; Hispanic-american Film; Contemporary Spanish-American Drama; Mayan Languages; Social Change in Latin America; Food Dilemmas of Latin America.*

✦ *Key Faculty*

Mercedes Lynn de Uriarte: Third world communication issues; popular culture; international journalism.
Admissions Information: (Address as above).

University of Wisconsin-Madison

Latin American/ Iberian Studies

University of Wisconsin-Madison
Latin American and Iberian Studies
1470 Van Hise Hall
1220 Linden Drive
Madison, WI 53706

Degree: M.A.

Phone 608/262-2811
Fax   608/265-5851

The degree is designed to provide an interdisciplinary study of Latin America, Spain, and Portugal. The program has no courses of its own except a core seminar on *Trends in Latin American Studies*. Instead, students enroll in courses from departments that offer subjects relevant to Latin America. These include Agriculture, Economics, Geography, History, and Political Science. *Course Highlights: People of the Andes Today; the Spanish-American Short Story; Multiracial Societies in Latin America; Latin American International Relations; Latin American Music.*

✦ *Key Faculty*

Barbara Stallings: U.S.-Latin American relations; international political economy.
Steve Stern: Social history of Latin America; colonial Latin America; Andes; Mexico.
Admissions Information: The Graduate School; University of Wisconsin-Madison; 228 Bascom Hall; 500 Lincoln Drive; Madison, WI 53706; Phone 608/262-2433.

Area Studies-Asia

Cornell University

Southeast Asia Program
180 Uris Hall
Cornell University
Ithaca, NY 14853-7601

Southeast Asia

Degrees: M.A., Grad Minor
Phone   607/255-2378
Fax   607/254-5000
E-mail   seap@cornell.edu

The Master of Arts in Southeast Asia Studies is an interdisciplinary degree program designed for individuals who plan on, or who are already engaged in professional careers that require a solid background in Southeast Asia, and for students who wish to acquire language/area studies proficiency before pursuing a disciplinary Ph.D. program. Students are required to achieve proficiency in one or more Southeast Asian language as well as focus on a particular region of Southeast Asia. Students have the opportunity to work and study with faculty members engaged in teaching and research on such varied fields as anthropology, Asian studies, agricultural economics, government, history, linguistics, and rural sociology. The program also offers instruction in many Southeast Asian languages including Burmese, Cebuano, Indonesian, Javanee, Hkmer, Tagalog, Thai, and Vietnamese. *Course Highlights: Anthropological Approaches to Study of Buddhism in Asia; Cultural History of Vietnam.*

Admissions Information: (Address as above).

Development/
International Relations

―――――◆◆――――

American University

International Development Program
School of International Service
Hurst Hall, Room 212
Washington, DC 20016-8040

Development

Degrees: M.A., M.S., Ph.D.

Phone   202/885-1660
Fax   202/885-1695

Active since 1975, this program sees development as an ethical, political, and technical endeavor. With community focus in both its curricula and its organization, the program stresses equity as a central objective. Training is offered in both micro and macro-level analyses that link theory and research with practical skills and action. As with many development programs, the approach is multidisciplinary.

American University offers two Master's degrees: a multidisciplinary program in International Development (M.A.I.D.) and a more applied program focusing specifically on Development Management (M.S.D.M.). There is also a Ph.D. degree in International Studies offered by the School of International Service. In addition to a variety of different concentrations to choose from, the core of the program(s) emphasizes understanding major theories of development, major development-related institutions, and critical evaluation of current issues and problems. Students also have the opportunity to participate in organizations actively involved in academic and program policy, community and professional programs, and social affairs. A student-run micro-enterprise (S.M.A.L.L.) serves as a hands-on learning laboratory on and off campus. *Course Highlights: Anthropology of Development; The Political Economy of African Crisis; Women in the Economy; International Environment and Politics.*

✦ Key Faculty

Robin Broad: Political economy of natural resources; sustainable development; North-South relations; Philippines, Indonesia.
Other interesting faculty: Steve Arnold, Deborah Brautigam, Fantu Cheru, John Richardson, Vidyamali Samarasinghe
Admissions Information: Office of Graduate Affairs and Admissions; The American University; 4400 Massachusetts Avenue, NW; Washington, DC 20016-8111; Phone 202/885-1098.

Clark University

Development

Program for International Development
    and Social Change (ID)
950 Main Street
Worcester, MA 01610-1477

Degree: M.A.

Phone   508/793-7201
Fax   508/793-8820

The M.A. in International Development has particular strengths in the areas of resource management, the environment, project design and implementation, women and development, and rural socio-economic change. It offers a grassroots focus on communities, villages, households, local institutions, and their linkages to broader economic, ecological, and political concerns. There is also a strong emphasis on Eastern Asia, with research activities in this region. As an interdisciplinary program, ID has a core teaching faculty of four people, drawing on an additional ten or more faculty from constituent departments. The M.A. involves a year of course work plus a thesis. Students often stretch the workload over two years, taking time for internships or research assistantships. *Course Highlights: Local Action/Global Change; African Crisis; Ecology and Economy of Third World Societies.*

✦ Key Faculty

Richard Ford: African history; resource management; participation; sustainable development.
Ann Seidman: Regional economics; African development; project analysis; development theory; role of the state in the development process.
Barbara Thomas-Slayter: Director, ID; local institutions and organizations; women and public policy; peasant-state relations; gender issues.
Admissions Information: (Address as above).

Cornell University

International Development Studies

Cornell University offers many programs within the area of International Development Studies, although there is no department with that title. We recommend a number of these programs in this guide, but there are many more. Due to the interdisciplinary nature of many of the programs, faculty we recommend in one program may teach in others. The publication, *International Development Studies at*

Cornell University describes all of the programs. It is produced by the Cornell International Institute for Food, Agriculture, and Development (CIIFAD): CIIFAD Publications; Box 14 Kennedy Hall; Cornell University; Ithaca, NY 14853-4203.

Institute of Development Studies

Development Studies

Institute of Development Studies
at the University of Sussex
Brighton BN1 9RE, UK

Degrees: M.A. (Gender and Devel.),
M.Phil., D.Phil.
Phone +44 273 606 261
Fax +44 273 691 647 or 621 202

Founded in 1966, the Institute of Development Studies emphasizes Third World development and political economy. A new Food Security Unit was established at the IDS in 1989. This move was designed to give greater coherence to the IDS's long-standing program of work on food issues and to lay the foundation for an expansion of research, teaching, and commissioned studies in a field of great and growing concern. The research and teaching program of the Food Security Unit is largely focused on sub-Saharan Africa in the following four areas: poverty reduction, sustainable development, and the rural sector; human resources; government, market, and society; and productive enterprise and its context. *Course Highlights: Statistics for Development Policy; Rural Research and Rural Policy; Food Security in Africa: Policy, Planning, and Interventions.*

✦ Key Faculty

Susanna Davies: Deputy Director, IDS; political economics; local food monitoring systems; indigenous coping strategies used by different producers (cultivators and pastoralists) during droughts; local and regional food security interventions in sub-Saharan Africa.

Reginald Green: Political economics; development policy; human condition of poor people; structural adjustment; economic cooperation among developing countries; human and economic costs of war in sub-Saharan Africa; external debt.

Melissa Leach: Social anthropology; geography; environmental aspects of rural development; gender issues.

Simon Maxwell: Rural development; agricultural economics; farming systems; agricultural development; food policy; impact of food aid.

Hans Singer: Economics; North-South relations; debt and adjustment problems; industrialization strategies; child development; food aid; terms of trade.

Admissions Information: Postgraduate Admissions; Sussex House; University of Sussex; Falmer, Brighton BN1 9RH; England; Phone +44 273 678 412; Fax +44 273 678 335; E-mail admissions@uk.ac.sussex.admin.

San Francisco State University

International Relations

San Francisco State University
Department of International Relations
1600 Holloway Avenue
San Francisco, CA 94132

Degrees: B.A., M.A.

Phone   415/338-2055
Fax   415/338-1980

San Francisco State University offers an interdisciplinary degree: courses in anthropology, women's studies, development, and others are cross-referenced within the forum of international relations. It covers a wide range of subjects, and students are encouraged to take advantage of the different disciplines. Because of its diverse base, students get an unusually broad perspective of international affairs, one that does not focus solely on state-to-state relations.

✦ *Key Faculty*

Raymond Miller: Political economy; Third World development.
Admissions Information: (Address as above).

University of Wisconsin, Madison

Development

University of Wisconsin, Madison
Land Tenure Center
1357 University Ave
Madison, WI 53715

Degree: Ph.D.
Phone   608/262-3412
Fax   608/262-2141
E-Mail landtenure.center@
        mail.adminwisc.edu

This is a widely interdisciplinary program that is both problem- and theory-oriented, designed to train social scientists for careers in development in poor countries. Through the Center, which administers the program, students have the opportunity to concentrate on issues of land tenure, agrarian reform, the impact of tenure change on women, and other areas of rural development and resource management. Academic advisers may be selected from quite a diverse array of disciplines, including agricultural economics, anthropology, business, rural sociology and sociology, political science, law, natural resources/forestry, journalism, history, geography, and nutritional sciences.

Those applying to the program should already hold a Master's degree in a discipline pertinent to development. Upon admission, students plan their own course work with an adviser and two other faculty members. A total of five faculty members eventually form the committee that administers the student's final thesis defense. While each program of study differs, students select courses that satisfy common guidelines. These include interdisciplinary seminars, courses from the major discipline, electives from secondary disciplines, research design/methodology/statistics, and thesis research.

✦ Key Faculty

Richard Barrows: Economics and tenure reform; Africa.

Susana Lastarria-Cornhiel: Agrarian reform; gender issues; Latin America; Eastern Europe.

Edward Friedman: Politics of tenure change; China.

Timothy Moermond: Ecology; conservation biology; Africa; the Caribbean.

Steven Hendrix: Legal aspects of tenure change; Latin America.

David Stanfield: Sociology of tenure change; Latin America; Eastern Europe.

Admissions Information: Ph.D. in Development Program; (Address as above).

OTHER PROGRAMS

Centro de Ecologia y Desarrollo
Apdo. Postal 11-440
Colonia Hipodromo-Condesa
Mexico, D.F. CP 06100
✦ *Key Faculty:* **David Barkin**

No degrees granted
Research possible
Phone   +52 55 753 604

Columbia University
Graduate School of Arts and Sciences
107 Low Library
New York, NY 10027

Degree: M.A.
Phone   212/854-4737

Harvard University
Social Change and Development Program
Department of Anthropology
Cambridge, MA 02138
✦ *Key Faculty:* **David Maybury-Lewis,
Pauline Peters, Parker Shipton**

Degree: M.A.
Phone   617/495-2246

Institute of Social Studies
PO Box 29776
The Hague 2502 LT
The Netherlands

Degrees: M.A., M.Phil., Ph.D.
         (Development Studies)
Phone: +31 704 260 460

University of Denver
Graduate School of
International Studies
Denver, CO 80208
✦ *Key Faculty:* **George Demartino,
Jendayi Frazer, David Goldfischer,
Ilene Grabel, Micheline Ishay**

Degree: M.A.
Phone   303/871-2544
Fax   303/871-2456

Economics

American University

Economics

American University
Department of Economics
4400 Massachusetts Avenue, NW
Washington, DC 20016-8029

Degrees: M.A., Ph.D.

Phone   202/885-3770
Fax   202/885-3790

The highlighted faculty members support the political economy track of the Ph.D. program, one of two possible courses of study at American. The four M.A. programs are: development banking, financial economics for public policy, economics, and applied economics. Fields of study include, but are not limited to: economic development, international economics, comparative economics, labor economics, public economies, economic history, political economy, economics of gender, and environmental economics. *Course Highlights: Foreign Assistance and Economic Development; Economics of World Regions; Economic Development Policy.*

✦ Key Faculty

Robert Blecker: International trade; economic growth.
Maria Floro: Agricultural economics; women; credit markets; development.
Robin Hahnel: Comparative economic systems; environmental economics.
Mieke Meurs: Women and development; worker self-management and the historical experiences of the Soviet Union; Eastern Europe; China, Cuba.
Larry Sawers: Development economics; U.S. economic history; regional and agricultural development.
Howard Wachtel: Labor economics; world economy; economic history.
John Willoughby: Imperialism; radical political economy.
Jon Wisman: Economic history and thought; workplace democracy.
Admissions Information: American University; Graduate Affairs and Admissions; 4400 Massachusetts Avenue, NW; Washington, DC 20016; Phone 202/885-3770.

Franklin and Marshall College   Economics

Franklin and Marshall College
Department of Economics
Lancaster, PA 17604

Degree: B.A.
Phone   717/291-3916
Fax   717/399-3969

The Economics Department at Franklin and Marshall College is one of the more progressive undergraduate economics departments. Students can fashion a curriculum in Gender and Race Economics, Political Economy, Labor Economics, Marxian Economics, and the History of Economics. *Course Highlights: Women and the U.S. Economy; History of Economic Thought; Economic Development.*

✦ *Key Faculty*

Antonio Callari: Marxian economics; gender; race; urban reconstruction.
Sean Flaherty: Labor economics; industrial relations.
Admissions Information: Franklin and Marshall College; Admissions Office; PO Box 3003; Lancaster, PA 17604-3003.

New School for Social Research   Economics

New School for Social Research
Department of Economics
Graduate School
65 Fifth Avenue
New York, NY 10003

Degrees: M.A., Ph.D.

Phone   212/229-5717
Fax   212/229-5724
E-mail   pezeshkp@
newschool.edu

The New School Economics Department offers a non-conventional economics curriculum, focusing on mainstream and Marxian economics. The five fields of study for the Ph.D. program are macroeconomics and policy, international studies, structural change and transformation, conflict and inequality, and the history of economic thought. *Course Highlights: Political Economy of the Environment; Third World in the World Economy; Labor Economics; Political Economy of Gender.*

✦ *Key Faculty*

John Eatwell: Labor markets; macroeconomic policy.
David Gordon: Labor economics; relationship between U.S. economic changes and changing work relations.

William Milberg: Income inequality; social structure of accumulation; international trade; technology change; methodology of economics.
Anu Shaikh: Marxian economics; financial markets; business cycles.
Lance Taylor: Development; structural adjustment policy; environmental economics.
Admissions Information: Graduate Faculty Admissions; New School for Social Research; 65 Fifth Avenue, Room 110; New York, NY 10003; Phone 800/523/5411.

University of California, Berkeley

Economics

Department of Economics
549 Evans Hall #3880
University of California
Berkeley, CA 94720-3880

Degrees: B.A., Ph.D.
Phone 510/642-0822 (Main)
Fax   510/642-6615
E-mail maindept.econ@
       uclink.berkeley.edu

The Department of Economics organizes its courses into three broad categories: economic theory and econometrics; applications and institutions; and economic history and history of economic thought. *Graduate Course Highlights: Labor Economics; Economic Development and Planning; Economic Demographics.*

✦ *Key Faculty*

Pranab Bardhan: Economic development; international economics; political economy; institutional economics.
Clair Brown: Director, Institute of International Relations; unemployment; income support systems; standards of living in the U.S. since 1918; employment systems in the U.S. and Japan.
Michael Reich: Political economy; labor economics; racial discrimination.
Admissions Information: (Graduate or Undergraduate) Admissions; 543 Evans Hall #3880; University of California; Berkeley, CA 94720-3880; Phone 510/642-6674.

University of California, Riverside

Economics

Department of Economics
University of California
Riverside, CA 92521-0427

Degrees: M.A., Ph.D.
Phone   909/787-5037
Fax   909/787-5685

The program in Political Economy and International Development is designed to prepare students for research and teaching in academic institutions as well as for research and counseling in business, trade unions, and government agencies in the United States and in other countries (including the Third World). Areas of concentration include economic development, comparative systems, international economics, public finance, labor economics, history of economic thought, monetary and financial economics, and economics and political economy. *Course Highlights: Political Economy of Development Colloquia; Econometrics Colloquia; Economic Theory Colloquia.*

✦ *Key Faculty*

Susan Carter: American economic history; labor economics; unemployment; wages, compensation, and labor costs; discrimination.
Gary Dymski: Financial intermediation; monetary macroeconomics; political economy.
David Fairris: Labor economics; political economy.
Keith Griffin: Poverty and inequality in the Third Word; China.
Robert Pollin: Macroeconomics; alternative approaches to money and finance; political economy.
Other interesting faculty: Susan Carter and Gary Dymski.
Admissions Information: (Address as above; zip 92521-0208); Phone 909/787-3313; Fax 909/787-2238.

University of Massachusetts Economics

University of Massachusetts
Department of Economics
Thompson Hall
Amherst, MA 01003

Degrees: B.A., M.A., Ph.D.

Phone   413/545-2590
Fax   413/545-2921

The program includes both Marxian and other forms of radical political economy as well as more conventional approaches. Program strengths are in economic development, labor economics, economic history, the theory of economic institutions, and non-neoclassical approaches, including feminist theory. The Center for Popular Economics, located in the department, offers workshops and crash courses in economics for progressive activists. *Course Highlights: Political Economy of the Environment; The Political Economy of Women; Economic Development.*

✦ Key Faculty

Samuel Bowles: Microeconomics; theory of institutions; economic advisor for unions and other groups in South Africa.
James Boyce: Development economics; environmental economics.
James Crotty: Macroeconomy; integration of complementary analytical strengths of the Marxian and Keynesian traditions in macrotheory.
Carmen Diana Deere: Latin American agricultural development; women and development; peasant household economics; agrarian reform; organization of production in the transition to socialism.
Gerald Epstein: Determinants of central bank policy in open economies; political economy of international credit relations; political economy of capital controls.
Diane Flaherty: Comparative economic systems; worker self-management emphasizing the process of Eastern European economic reform.
Nancy Folbre: Women's issues in the fields of economic history and development.
Herbert Gintis: Microfoundations of political economy; development and application of microeconomic theory towards a new understanding of the link between competitive markets and the structure of economic power.
Carol Heim: City-building, land values, and property developers in different historical contexts.
David Kotz: Economic transition in the former USSR; Marxian economic theory; macroeconomics; economic history.
Mohan Rao: Development economics; economic history; environment-economy links in India.
Stephen Resnick: Methodology; class analysis.
Lisa Saunders: Transportation; labor economics.
Richard Wolff: Marxian economics; postmodern approach to the modernism of prevailing economic theories; class aspects of the problems of contemporary capitalism.
Admissions Information: (Address as above).

University of Notre Dame   Economics

University of Notre Dame
Department of Economics
Notre Dame, IN 46556

Degrees: B.A., M.A., Ph.D.
Phone   219/631-6335
Fax   219/631-8209

The economics graduate program at Notre Dame is distinguished by an openness to alternative theoretical approaches and methodologies, and by a commitment to research related to issues of economic and social justice. Faculty recognize the importance of intellectual diversity and actively support it. Ideas from the neoclassical, post-Keynesian, neo-Marxian, and institutionalist traditions are developed critically. Areas of specialization currently include development, history of thought and methodology, industrial organization, international economics, labor, money and financial institutions, public finance, and theory. Students also have access to the Kellogg Institute for International Studies, which brings in Latin Americanists for research, education, and outreach. *Course Highlights: History of Economic Thought; Problems in Political Economy; Seminar in Alternative Labor Theories and Applied Research.*

✦ Key Faculty

Amitava Dutt: Growth and distribution theory; Keynesian and post-Keynesian macroeconomic theory; classical political economy; development economics; international economics.

Candace Howes: Industrial organization; trade and industrial policy.

David Ruccio: Third World development; socialist planning; international political economy; Marxian economics; methodology.

Charles Wilber: Development, political economy; methodology.

Admissions Information: The Graduate School; University of Notre Dame; Notre Dame, IN 46556-5602; Phone 219/631-7706; Fax 219/631-6630.

University of Southern Maine　Economics

University of Southern Maine
Department of Economics
96 Falmouth Street
Portland, ME 04103

Degrees: B.A., B.S., M.A. (in Public Policy and Management)
Phone　207/780-4293
Fax　207/780-4662
E-mail　medley@usm.maine.edu

The University of Southern Maine Economics Department offers close contact with a very active, intellectually and culturally diverse faculty that continues to grow. Program strengths include economic theory (political economy and feminist economics), labor (including gender and discrimination), international economic development, industrial organization (including environmental and technology), and economic systems (especially East Asian economies). *Course Highlights: Economics of Gender and Discrimination; Urban Economics; Economic System of the Soviet Union.*

✦ Key Faculty

Joseph Medley: Department Chair.
Admissions Information: University of Southern Maine; 37 College Avenue; Gorham, ME 04038; Phone 207/780-5670; Toll free 800/800-4USM*5670.

University of Utah

Director of Graduate Studies
Department of Economics-308 BUC
University of Utah
Salt Lake City, UT 84112

Economics

Degrees: M.A., M.S., M.Statistics, Ph.D.
Phone   801/581-7481
Fax   801/585-5649
E-mail   program@econ.sbs.utah.edu

Both orthodox and heterodox approaches to economics are integral parts of the broad and intellectually varied graduate Economics Department at the University of Utah. The department offers a program in applied economics, along with other areas of specialization, including regional and urban economics, public finance, natural-resource and environmental economics, economic history, quantitative analysis in economics, industrial organization, monetary economics, human resource economics, and others. Students should note that not all fields are offered every year. *Course Highlights: Economic Development of the Middle East; Political Economy of Women; Poverty and Income Maintenance; Environment and Development.*

✦ Key Faculty

Nilufer Cagatay: International trade; economics of gender; women and development.
E.K. Hunt: Political economy; history of economic doctrine.
Peter Philips: Labor; collective bargaining; history; discrimination.
Admissions Information: (Address as above).

OTHER PROGRAMS

Harvard University
Department of Economics
Littauer 200
Cambridge, MA 02138

Degree: Ph.D.
Phone   617/495-2144

✦ Key Faculty: Stephen Marglin, Juliet Schor

Education

Guilford College

Education Studies

Guilford College
Education Studies Department
5800 West Friendly Avenue
Greensboro, NC 27410

Degree: B.A.
Phone   910/316-2270
Fax   910/316-2949
E-mail   byrnesrs@rascal.guilford.edu

Guilford College has a newly redesigned teacher education program. Based on Quaker values, courses and internships are designed to prepare thoughtful educational leaders capable of effecting change. Students are required to double major. In the secondary program, students earn teaching credentials in English, Social Studies, Spanish, French, or Physical Education. *Course Highlights: East Asia Education; Early Childhood Education; Field Study and Cross Cultural Education.*

✦ *Key Faculty*

Ron Byrnes: Global education; multicultural education; educational reform.
Admissions Information: Office of Admissions; (Address as above); Phone 800/992-7759.

University of California, Berkeley

Education

Graduate School of Education
1600 Tolman Hall #1670
University of California
Berkeley, CA 94720-1670

Degrees: Ed.D., M.A., Ph.D.
Phone   510/642-0841
Fax   510/642-4808
E-mail   gse-info@
         maillink.berkeley.edu

Berkeley's Graduate School of Education's central mission is to link knowledge and research on education with efforts to improve teaching and learning in schools. To facilitate this mission, credential programs are integrated into five academic divisions: Educational Administration; Educational Psychology; Education in Language and Literacy; Education in Mathematics, Science, and Technology; and Social and Cultural Studies in Education. Educational Administration serves students who pursue leadership careers in school administration and higher education. Students who study Educational Psychology look at psychological theory combined with educational practice. The Division of Educational Psychology is organized into a major research program (Human Development) and two professional programs (School Psychology and Developmental Teacher Education). The Division of Education in Language and Literacy focuses on research in issues related to the education of diverse populations, preparing students to work with individuals who aren't served well by existing educational institutions. Graduate preparation in Education in Mathematics, Science, and Technology emphasizes the search for fresh insights into major educational problems, focusing on cognitive science and the resources of modern technology. Two national research centers are housed at the Graduate School of Education: the National Center for Research in Vocational Education and the National Center for the Study of Writing and Literacy. *Course Highlights: Economic Development and Education in the Third World; Evaluation in the Schools; Human and Machine Learning.*

✦ Key Faculty

John Hurst: Popular education and participation; adult education for democratic social change; national and international environmental justice.
Admissions Information: (Address as above).

University of California, Santa Cruz

Education

Board of Studies in Education
1156 High Street
University of California
Santa Cruz, CA 95064

Degrees: M.A., Grad Certificate

Phone   408/459-3712
Fax   408/459-4618

The graduate programs in education seek to prepare informed, articulate, analytical leaders of educational reform within schools and the community. Two programs are offered by the Education Board: the Graduate Certificate in Education and the M.A. in Education. The Graduate Certificate program offers the multiple subject teaching credential for elementary school teachers and the single-subject teaching credential for secondary teachers. It also encompasses CLAD (Crosscultural, Language, and Academic Development), which emphasizes a unique understanding of the rich cultural and linguistic diversity in the California public schools. UC Santa Cruz has a strong emphasis on multicultural education. *Course Highlights: Minorities in the Schooling Process; Teaching Learning and Schooling in Social Context.*

The Master of Arts program focuses on preparing researchers and teacher educators in theory and research relevant to teaching and learning in a culturally, linguistically, and socially diverse society. Students are expected to choose an area of emphasis related to faculty specializations, which include language and literacy; bilingual and multicultural education; sociocultural theory; education in mathematics, science and technology; cognitive, emotional, and human development; aesthetics education; and the anthropology of education. *Course Highlights: Immigrants and Education; Teaching, Learning and Schooling in Social Context.*

Admissions Information: UCSC-Division of Graduate Studies; 399 Applied Sciences Building; University of California; Santa Cruz, CA 95064; Phone 408/459-2301.

University of Denver

International Relations

Center for Teaching International Relations
University of Denver
2201 South Gaylord Street
Denver, CO 80208-0268

Degree: M.A.
Phone 303/871-3106 or
           800/967-2847
Fax   303/871-2906 or
           303/871-2456

Recognizing that today's educator needs to have knowledge of how the world works and the skills to deliver that information to students, the Center for Teaching International Relations (CTIR) has created a Master of Arts program. This program includes substantive background in international studies, social and political issues analysis, and curriculum development in the participant's chosen area. This program is designed to enhance teacher skills in three areas: Teaching major substantive world issues, trends, and themes in the precollegiate classroom; Planning, developing, and evaluating curricula related to the issues that confront humankind; and Developing practical classroom strategies that provide meaningful learning experiences for students in all disciplines. *Course Highlights: Cultural Foundations of Education; World Politics for Precollegiate Teachers.*

✦ Key Faculty

Peter Downing: Director, CTIR M.A. program and publications division; environment and water rights; Ghana.

Admissions Information: University of Denver; Graduate Admissions Office; Mary Reed Building Room #5A; Denver, CO 80208.

———————◆———————

University of San Francisco   Education

University of San Francisco
School of Education
2130 Fulton Street
San Francisco, CA 94117-1080

Degrees: M.A., Ed.D.

Phone   415/666-6525
Fax   415/666-2677

The School of Education offers programs in four distinctive areas. The Counseling Psychology program prepares professional counselors and psychologists for effective performance in the helping professions. Students take part in field work that includes counseling theory and practice, assessment, and consultation. Students in the Curriculum and Instruction program learn about curriculum design and supervision, instructional leadership and technology, evaluation, research, and instructional design. International and Multicultural Education focuses on current and future educational issues and the needs of an increasingly multicultural society—nationally and around the globe. The school is committed to preparing leaders from ethnic, cultural, and linguistic groups underrepresented in higher education. The program in Organization and Leadership prepares administrators and leaders in education, industry, business, health and human services, and government. Students look at relationships among individuals, organizations, and society so that they are prepared to meet the education and training-related challenges to revitalize those organizations. The Teacher Education program is designed to prepare exemplary classroom teachers, ready and able to assume duties in multicultural and multilingual classrooms. *Course Highlights: Crosscultural Literacy; Moral Development; Student Teaching.*

Admissions Information: Office of the Dean; (Address as above).

OTHER PROGRAMS

International Education
Teachers College
Columbia University
New York, NY 10027

Degrees: M.A., M.E., Ph.D.
Phone   212/678-3184

Teacher Education Program
University of Denver
2135 East Wesley Avenue, Room 205
Denver, CO 80208
✦ *Key Faculty:* Gary Lichtenstein

Degree: Teacher Licensure
Phone   303/871-2519
Fax   303/871-3422

Mills College
Department of Education
5000 MacArthur Blvd.
Oakland, CA 94613-1301
✦ *Key Faculty:* Vicki LaBoskey, Anna Richert

Degree: M.A.
Phone   510/430-2118
Fax   510/430-3379

Environment

Evergreen State College

Evergreen State College
Graduate Program in Environmental Studies
Olympia, WA 98505

Environmental Studies

Degree: M.E.S.

Phone   206/866-6000 ext. 6707

The Master's in Environmental Science at Evergreen consists of three closely integrated components: required core studies in the social, natural, and physical sciences; electives that provide more specialized training in subjects related to environmental studies; and thesis work that often takes the form of applied research. Evergreen specifically offers water quality, marine and environmental chemistry laboratories, as well as a scanning electron microscope, a natural history museum, an herbarium, and an experimental farm. *Course Highlights: Political, Economic, and Ecological Processes; Environmental Philosophy and Ethics; Environmental Issues in Latin America.*

Admissions Information: Admissions Office; The Evergreen State College; Olympia, WA 98505-0002; Phone 206/866-6000, Ext. 6170.

Friends World Program

Friends World Program
Southampton Campus
Long Island University
Southampton, NY 11968

Environmental Studies

Degree: B.A. Interdisciplinary Studies

Phone   516/283-4000
Fax   516/283-4081

Long Island University's Friends World Program is an international college specializing in experiential education. It offers an interdisciplinary liberal arts program that includes a concentration in natural sciences in which students can focus on, among other areas, Agriculture/Resource Management and Ecology/Environmental Studies. Students combine seminars and guided independent work in the United States and at least two other cultures outside of their own to complete the degree. Centers are located in New York, Israel, India, England, Costa Rica, Kenya, Japan, and China.

✦ *Key Faculty*

Corey Dolgon: American culture; cultural studies; poverty; homeless and welfare action groups.
Hugh McGuinness: Sustainable agriculture and development; ecological management; local organic farms.

Kathleen Modrowski: Anthropology.
Admissions Information: (Address as above).

University of California, Berkeley

Conservation Resource Studies

Conservation Resource Studies
College of Natural Resources
Department of Environmental Science,
    Policy, and Management
112 Giannini Hall #3100
University of California
Berkeley, CA 94720-3100

Degree: B.S.

Phone   510/642-6730
Fax   510/642-6632

The Conservation Resource Studies program allows students to construct an area of emphasis around environmental issues. The program has a strong history of student participation in decision-making, and is at the forefront of preparing students for work within environmental causes and organizations. *Course Highlights: Forest and Wildland Resource Conservation; Ecosystem Ecology; Environmental Law and Regulation.*

✦ Key Faculty

Donald Dahlsten: Biological control of forest and urban tree insects; population dynamics of bark beetles and defoliators; impact of insectivorous birds on forest insects.
Joseph Hancock: Soil-borne plant pathogens; biological control; ecology of root-microbe associations; fungus physiology.
John Hurst: Popular education and participation; adult education for democratic social change; national and international environmental justice.
Carolyn Merchant: Environmental history; environmental philosophy and ethics; women and the environment; environmental movement.
Other interesting faculty: Claudia Carr, Arnold Schultz, and David Wood.
Admissions Information: (Address as above).

University of California, Berkeley

Environment

College of Natural Resources
Department of Environmental Science,
    Policy, and Management
145 Mulford Hall #3114
University of California
Berkeley, CA 94720-3114

Degrees: M.A., Ph.D.

Phone   510/642-6410
Fax   510/643-5438
E-mail   espmgradproginfo@
           nature.berkeley.edu

The recently consolidated Department of Environmental Science, Policy, and Management offers degrees in Entomology, Plant Pathology, Soil Science, Wildland Resource Science, as well as a Master of Forestry. The department hopes to have a new integrated graduate program to be offered Fall of 1996. *Course Highlights: Forest and Wildland Resource Conservation; Forest Ecology; Environmental Law and Regulation.*

✦ Key Faculty

Louise Fortmann: Sociology of natural resource management; gender; property rights.
Admissions Information: (Address as above).

University of California, Santa Cruz

Environmental Studies

Environmental Studies Board
University of California
Santa Cruz, CA 95064

Degrees: B.A., Ph.D.
Grad. Phone   408/459-4837
Ugrad. Phone 408/459-3718
Joint Fax   408/459-3518
Grad. E-mail nama@zzyx.ucsc.edu

The Board of Environmental Studies offers an interdisciplinary major program leading to a Bachelor of Arts degree. The major focuses on the sustainability of cultural and ecological systems through conservation, management, agriculture, planning, policy, development, and restoration. There is a geographical emphasis at the regional level, a focus on non-urban and wildlands, and a concern about biodiversity and about environmental, social, and economic well being. The degree can also be combined with biology, economics, or Latin

American and Latino studies. *Course Highlights: Ecodevelopment; Political Economy of Sustainable Agriculture in Latin America; Sustainable Soil Management.*

The Ph.D. program is disciplinary and interdisciplinary, focusing on the concept of ecological sustainability and the fields of political economy and sustainability, conservation biology, and agroecology. Graduates will specialize in one of the fields (with a disciplinary or subdisciplinary specialization), but be conversant in all three. The program emphasizes the physical, biological, and socioeconomic factors affecting sustainable uses of agricultural and wildlands ecosystems, and examines the conflicts that often arise between social objectives and economic welfare on the one hand and conservation objectives on the other. *Course Highlights: Agroecology and Sustainable Agriculture; Advanced Insect Ecology; Advanced Readings in Political Economy and Sustainability.*

✦ **Key Faculty**

Stephen Gliessman: Agroecology; sustainable agriculture; tropical agriculture; ecology; natural history; California vegetation.

David Goodman: Modern food systems; agri-biotechnologies; sustainable agriculture; environmental policy; rural development in Third World societies.

Graduate Admissions Information: Division of Graduate Studies; Environmental Studies Board; 399 Applied Sciences Building; University of California; Santa Cruz, CA 95064; Phone 408/459-2301.

Undergraduate Admissions Information: Environmental Studies Board; Room 226 College 8; University of California; Santa Cruz, CA 95064; Phone 408/459-3718.

Ethnic Studies

California State University

California State University
Department of Chicano Studies
King Hall C3095
5151 State University Drive
Los Angeles, CA 90032-8221

Chicano Studies

Degree: M.A.

Phone   213/343-2290 or 2190
Fax   213/343-5155

The Department of Chicano Studies offers a Master of Arts degree in Mexican-American Studies. Through course work within Chicano Studies and other departments, students are acquainted with a breadth of knowledge about Chicanos and are exposed to theoretical perspectives specific to this area of study. *Course Highlights: Chicano Psychological Issues; Chicano History; Chicano Literature.*

✦ *Key Faculty*

Francisco Balderrama: Chicano history.

Cornell University

Africana Studies and Research Center
Cornell University
310 Triphammer Road
Ithaca, NY 14850-2599

Africana Studies

Degrees: B.A., M.P.S.

Phone   607/255-4625
Fax   607/255-0784

The Africana Studies and Research Center offers a program of study that leads to an undergraduate degree through the College of Arts and Sciences and a graduate degree, the Master of Professional Studies (African, African-American), through the university's graduate school. Interdisciplinary instruction, field training, and research concentrate on the past and present characteristics, achievements, and problems of black people in Africa, in the New World, and particularly in the United States. The Africana Studies and Research Center hosts lectures and seminars to bring outstanding artists and scholars to share their insights on black life and culture, and assists students who are interested in pursuing their education at the advanced graduate level for teaching and research, law, medicine, public policy analysis and administration, and international affairs and development. *Course Highlights: History and Politics of Racism and Segregation; Swahili Literature; Women of Africa and of the Diaspora in Liberation Movements.*

✦ Key Faculty

Locksley Edmondson: Caribbean and African relations within the Third World movement; economics; international race relations.
Robert Harris: African American history; social and political movements.
James Turner: Black political sociology; racism and social analysis; urban community development; public policy.
Admissions Information: (Address as above).

Ohio State University — Black Studies

Department of Black Studies	Degrees: B.A., M.A.
Ohio State University	
486 University Hall	
230 North Oval Mall	Phone 614/292-3700
Columbus, OH 43210-1319	Fax 614/292-2293

Originally established as an academic division in 1969, Black Studies obtained formal department status in 1972 and has evolved into one of the largest, most dynamic, most effective, free-standing Black academic and research programs in the world. The primary goal is to stimulate teaching and research about the Black experience in the U.S., Africa, and throughout the African Diaspora, and to encourage students and others to assess various strategies for advancing human progress through the examination of the worldwide struggle for Black freedom. The department also emphasizes the importance of community outreach and sponsors the Black Studies Community Extension Center, located at the heart of the historic African-American community. *Course Highlights: African Protest Movements; Black American Family; Black Role Models: Racism and Sexism.*

✦ Key Faculty

William Nelson, Jr.: Black politics; urban politics; race and ethnic relations; public policy.
Admissions Information: Admissions Office; The Ohio State University; Lincoln Tower; 1800 Cannon Drive; Columbus, OH 43210-1200; Phone 614/292-3980.

San Francisco State University   Ethnic Studies

San Francisco State University
School of Ethnic Studies
1600 Holloway Avenue
San Francisco, CA 94132

Degree: M.A.

Phone   415/338-1859
Fax   415/338-1739

The Master of Arts in Ethnic Studies is an interdisciplinary graduate degree program that provides a comparative foundation in ethnic studies and a specific focus on either Asian Americans, African Americans, Latinos or American Indian peoples. This degree is flexible in nature and is inclusive rather than exclusive of employment opportunities. Options for employment include ethnic-oriented teaching and research, community and multi-cultural resource development, as well as practical application in the business and technical fields. Program graduates are also eligible to apply for teaching positions in the California community colleges in ethnic studies and related fields. *Course Highlights: History of U.S. People of Color; Ethnic Community Practicum.*

✦ *Key Faculty*

Jose Cuellar: Director, La Raza Studies.
Admissions Information: (Address as above); Phone 415/338-1859.

University of Arizona   American Indian Studies

American Indian Studies
The University of Arizona
Harvill Building Room 430
Tucson, AZ 85721

Degree: M.A.

Phone   520/621-7108
Fax   520/621-7952

The American Indian Studies program offers concentrations in three areas: American Indian Law and Policy, American Indian Languages and Literature, and American Indian Societies and Cultures. American Indian Law and Policy focuses on the development of federal Indian law and policy from the Europeans' first contact with Native Americans to the present. American Indian Languages and Literature gives students insight from Native American perspectives. By exploring native writers and languages, students see how Native American languages and literature are used in cultural contexts. American

Indian Societies and Cultures explores world views, institutions, and socio-cultural characteristics of tribal life in North America. Students also have options on how they obtain their M.A. They can write a thesis, have a comprehensive written exam and complete additional course work, or conduct a research project. *Course Highlights: Dynamics of Indian Societies; Race and Public Policy; Hopi Language and Culture.*

✦ Key Faculty

N. Scott Momaday: Kiowa; English; author of *House Made of Dawn* and *The Way to Rainy Mountain.*
David Wilkins: Politics of American Indians and specific theoretical approaches employed by policy-makers; Indian policy studies.
Ofelia Zepeda: Structure of the Tohono O'odham language and speech variation among speakers.
Admissions Information: (Address as above).

University of California, Berkeley

Ethnic Studies

Department of Ethnic Studies
508 A Barrows Hall #2570
University of California
Berkeley, CA 94720-2570

Degrees: B.A., M.A., Ph.D.

Phone   510/642-6643
Fax   510/642-6456

The program examines race in American life, focusing on African Americans, Asian Americans, Chicanos, and Native Americans. To gain a greater depth of understanding of America's racial diversity, students cover the histories, cultures, and communities of racial minorities in the United States and analyze the differences and similarities among the experiences of various racial minorities. The curriculum is taught by faculty from African American, Asian American, Chicano, and Native American Studies and faculty from the social science and humanities disciplines. *Course Highlights: Major Racial Minorities in the United States.*

✦ Key Faculty

Percy Hintzen: Political economy of the Third World; politics and ideology; Guyana, Trinidad and Tobago.
June Jordan: Women studies; Afro-American studies; author of *His Own Where* (National Book Award).

Beatriz Manz: Peoples and cultures of Central America; U.S. foreign policy in Central America.
Alex Saragoza: Chicano history; history of race and family; historical development of Mexican elites.
Ronald Takaki: Asian American history; American race relations.
Admissions Information: (Address as above).

University of California, Los Angeles

Afro-American Studies

Center for Afro-American Studies
160 Haines Hall
405 Hilgard Avenue AA02
University of California
Los Angeles, CA 90024-1545

Degrees: B.A., M.A.

Phone   310/825-3776
Fax   310/206-3421

The B.A. program in Afro-American Studies is designed to offer students an opportunity to study systematically the origins, experiences, and conditions of people of African descent. Students are required to select an area of concentration in anthropology, economics, English, history, philosophy, political science, psychology, or sociology and complete core courses in Afro-American Studies. *Course Highlights: Comparative Slavery Systems; Culture, Media, and Los Angeles.*

The M.A. is international in scope and focuses on African-origin cultures in the United States, the Caribbean, Central and South America. This interdisciplinary program gives students the opportunity to gain expertise in a traditional field as well as Afro-American Studies. The program provides a theoretical base of knowledge, methods of research, and a context for analyzing and interpreting the African diasporic experience, which can be invaluable either in further graduate study or a specific career. *Course Highlights: Afro-American Sociolinguistics: Black English; Political Economy of Race.*

Admissions Information: (Address as above).

University of California, Los Angeles

American Indian Studies

American Indian Studies Center
3220 Campbell Hall
Box 951548
University of California
Los Angeles, CA 90024-7060

Degree: M.A.

Phone   310/825-7315
Fax   310/206-7060

UCLA established the first Interdisciplinary Master of Arts program in American Indian Studies in 1982. Students take classes from the extensive variety of faculty and departments. To ensure that students explore various perspectives of American Indian issues, research and research methodologies are emphasized in this program. Upon graduation, students will be prepared to teach Native American studies and will have research skills to do original work. The M.A. program is associated with the American Indian Studies Center, which ranks among the top research centers of its kind. *Course Highlights: Native American Revitalization Movements; Cultural World Views of Native America; Indian Law.*

Admissions Information: (Address as above).

University of California, Los Angeles

Asian American Studies

Asian American Studies Center
3230 Campbell Hall
University of California
Los Angeles, CA 90024-1546

Degrees: B.A., M.A.

Phone   310/825-2974
Fax   310/206-9844

The undergraduate curriculum offers courses in Asian American history, psychology, sociology, anthropology, literature, film and media, women, and law. The program integrates the diverse experiences of a "history in progress" from the perspectives of native-born Asian Americans and Pacific Islanders to first generation women and men. *Undergraduate Course Highlights: Minority Group Politics; Folk Music of South Asia; Chinese Immigration.*

The graduate program offers training to students interested in teaching and research in Asian American communities. It is interdisciplinary with an emphasis on the history, politics, and culture of Asians in America. Students can work through the Asian American Studies Center for research, resource development and publications, and student/community projects. *Graduate Course Highlights: Critical Issues in U.S.-Asian Relations; Vietnamese-American Experience; Filipino-American Community Issues; Asian Americans and Public Policy.*

✦ **Key Faculty**

Don Nakanishi: Asian-Americans; political empowerment; education.
Admissions Information: (Address as above).

University of California, Santa Cruz

Latin American/Latino Studies

Latin American and Latino Studies
Merrill College
1156 High Street
University of California
Santa Cruz, CA 95064

Degrees: B.A., Undergrad Minor

Phone   408/459-4284
Fax   408/459-3125

The program in Latin American and Latino studies integrates the study of Chicano and Latino populations in the United States with the study of the history, political systems, social and economic structures, cultural expression, and complex ethnic heritage of Latin America and the Caribbean. Knowledge of Spanish or Portuguese, historical grounding in the forces that shaped "greater Latin America," and familiarity with contemporary Latin American and Latino issues are central to the major. Students choose one of two overlapping concentrations. Politics and Society emphasizes social science disciplines, drawing from anthropology, economics, history, politics, and sociology. Culture and Society concentrates on the arts and humanities and draws from anthropology, art history, history, music, and literature (including film). *Course Highlights: Latin American Land and Peasants; Political Change in the Third World; La Nueva Cancion Latinoamericana.*

✦ **Key Faculty**

Susanne Jonas: Comparative Latin American politics; political economy of development and underdevelopment; U.S. foreign policy; Central America, the Caribbean.
Admissions Information: Office of Admissions; University of California; Santa Cruz, CA 95064; Phone 408/459-4008.

University of Wisconsin   Afro-American Studies

University of Wisconsin
Afro-American Studies Department
4227 Humanities
455 N Park Street
Madison, WI 53706

Degrees: B.A., M.A.

Phone   608/263-1642
Fax   608/263-0805

The Department of Afro-American Studies offers students an opportunity to study aspects of black history, culture, and society in interdisciplinary models that reconstruct Afro-American life. It challenges students to examine critically facts and issues that are historically and currently relevant to the Afro-American experience. Students interested in a B.A. must complete 30 credits selected from three areas of concentration: Afro-American culture; Afro-American history; and Afro-American society. Students specialize in one of these areas but complete at least one class from each field. *Undergraduate Course Highlights: Blacks, Film, and Society; Critical and Theoretical Perspectives in Black Women's Writings.*

The Master of Arts program encourages students to employ innovative as well as conventional methods of scholarship that contribute to the development of Afro-American studies and to the diversification of other academic disciplines, communities, and institutions. With a strong emphasis on research and writing, the program prepares students for entry into Ph.D. programs and for professional positions in education and related fields. The faculty is committed to academic excellence and promotes interdisciplinary study in three major areas: culture, history, and society. *Graduate Course Highlights: Black Autobiography; History of Black Nationalism; The Education of Black Americans.*

✦ Key Faculty

Richard Ralston: Folklore; prisoner studies; comparative political movements; Southern African history; the Caribbean.

OTHER PROGRAMS

University of California, Davis   Degree: B.A.
Native American Studies
   ✦ *Key Faculty:* Stefono Varese   Phone   916/752-3237

Geography

Clark University

Graduate School of Geography
Clark University
950 Main Street
Worcester, MA 01610-1477

Geography

Degrees: M.S., Ph.D.

Phone   508/793-7337 or 7336
Fax   508/793-8881

Clark University has a reputation as a progressive school with a strong international focus. About 20% of its 2000 undergraduates and 800 post-graduates are from abroad. The Graduate School of Geography, founded in 1921, maintains an environmental emphasis. The school is closely linked to Clark University's George Perkins March Institute, a consortium of research centers and libraries focused on issues of human-environment relationships. The graduate geography program covers six main areas: cartography, cultural geography, environmental and resource geography, geomorphology/biogeography, regional/international development and political economy, and urban social and economic geography. *Course Highlights: Oceanic Islands; Gender Resources and Development; Agriculture in Third World Economies; Landscapes of the Middle East.*

✦ Key Faculty

Susan Hanson: Director, Graduate School of Geography; urban social and economic geography; urban labor markets; geography of women's employment.
Admissions Information: (Address as above).

Rutgers

Department of Geography
Rutgers, The State University of New Jersey
Lucy Stone Hall
PO Box 5080
New Brunswick, NJ 08903-5080

Geography

Degrees: M.A., M.S., Ph.D.

Phone   908/445-4103
Fax   908/445-0006

Rutgers University has the largest and most comprehensive geography graduate program in the region and one of the strongest research programs in the country. The majority of course and research opportunities are associated with physical geography, environmental geography, and social theory and geography. Faculty members are involved with many institutes and organizations, including:

Environmental and Occupational Health Services Institute, Water Resources Institute, Center for Urban Policy Research, and the Agricultural Experiment Station. Physical geography research currently focuses on landscape ecology, ground water and water supply, dynamics of the coastal zone, and process response modeling of beaches and dunes. Environmental geography research includes global environmental change, risk perception, development and underdevelopment, political ecology of Africa, and human responses to environmental hazards and disasters. Social geography and social theory research covers social, political, and economic restructuring in Central and Eastern Europe, housing, residential segregation and community control of land use, gender, and trans-Atlantic transfer of material culture.

✦ Key Faculty

Neil Smith: Urban geography; social theory; political economy; history of geography.
Admissions Information: Office of Graduate and Professional Admissions; Rutgers, The State University of New Jersey; Van Nest Hall; PO Box 5053; New Brunswick, NJ 08903-5053.

University of California, Berkeley   Geography

Department of Geography
501 McCone Hall #4740
University of California
Berkeley, CA 94720-4740

Degrees: B.A., M.A., Ph.D.

Phone 510/642-3903
Fax 510/642-3370

The undergraduate major in geography studies the various aspects of cultural, human, physical, and regional geography as well as cartography, quantitative methods, and field work. Students have the opportunity to look at the interlocking systems of the natural environment and the evaluation of natural resources; diverse historical, cultural, social, economic, and political structures and processes that affect the location and spatial organization of population groups and their activities; and significant geographical units, including cities, regions, nations, states or landscapes. *Undergraduate Course Highlights: The Political Economy and Historical Geography of Latin American Development; Local and Regional Transformation.*

On the graduate level, the Department of Geography offers training in physical, cultural, economic, urban, and regional geography focusing on the interrelationships between these specialties and related approaches in other fields. Systematic and regional specialization is recommended. Students are also encouraged to take classes in other departments, which would enhance their training as geographers. *Graduate Course Highlights: Cultural and Human Ecology; Economic Geography and Development Theory.*

✦ Key Faculty

Beatriz Manz: Director, Center for Latin American Studies; human and political geography; population migration; peasants; Latin America.
Bernard Nietschmann: Fourth World theory; cultural-political geography; tropical marine ecology; Latin America; the Pacific.
Allan Pred: Social theory; cultural studies; local and regional transformation.
Richard Walker: Industrial geography; economic development; urbanization; water resources; environmental regulation; Marxist theory; U.S.; California.
Michael Watts: Third World political economy, political ecology; development; peasant societies; social and cultural theory; U.S. agriculture; Africa.
Admissions Information: (Address as above).

University of California, Los Angeles

Geography

405 Hilgard Avenue (1255 Bunche Hall)
Department of Geography
University of California
Los Angeles, CA 90095-1524

Degrees: M.A., Ph.D.

Phone   310/825-1071

The areas of interest of faculty in Department of Geography include urban and regional development studies, spatial demography and social processes in the city, culture and environment in the modern world, physical geography, and biogeography. *Course Highlights: African Ecology and Development; Population Geography; Contemporary Issues in Urban Poverty Research.*

Admissions Information: (Address as above).

---◆---

University of Washington — Geography

Department of Geography
408 Smith Hall DP-10
University of Washington
Seattle, WA 98195

Degrees: M.A., Ph.D.
Phone 206/543-4915
Fax 206/543-3313
E-mail craigzb@u.washington.edu

The Geography Department at the University of Washington is one of the nation's leading centers for graduate training in industrial and economic geography, regional development and international area studies, urban and social geography, and cartography and geographic information systems. The program trains students for both empirical and theoretical research, emphasizing the application of research to contemporary problems. Students design their studies in one of four areas: urban, social and political geography; economic geography; area studies and international development studies; or cartography and geographic information systems. The department offers a less structured environment, more inviting of individual initiative and direction. *Course Highlights: The Geography of Cities; The Geography of Inequality; World Hunger and Resource Development.*

✦ Key Faculty

Victoria Lawson: Latin America; labor migration and workforce composition; development theory; regional development.
Lucy Jarosz: Agrarian and environmental change in the Third World; rural development theory; political economy; social theory; Africa.
Kathryne Mitchell: Urban geography; landscape and architecture; Pacific Rim migration; capital flow and China.
Admissions Information: Coordinator of Student Services; (Address as above); Phone 206/543-3246; E-mail rroth@u.washington.edu.

---◆---

University of Wisconsin-Madison — Geography

University of Wisconsin-Madison
Department of Geography
384 Science Hall
550 N. Park Street
Madison, WI 53706

Degree: M.S.

Phone 608/262-2138

The Graduate Department of Geography offers a broad range of programs in human, physical, regional, and historical geography as well as several classes in people/environment relations and a separate M.S. in cartography. Both the university and the city of Madison have an unusually large range of facilities for research in this field, including the Institute for Environmental Studies, a soil laboratory, and the State Historical Society Library. *Course Highlights: People, Land, and Food: Comparative Study of Agriculture Systems; Culture and Environment; Regional Cultures and Economies in the North American Past.*

✦ *Key Faculty*

Martin Lewis: Cultural geography; history of geographic thought; environmental degradation; Southeast Asia.

History

Columbia University   History

Columbia University
Department of History
611 Fayerweather
New York, NY 10027

Degrees: M.A., M.Phil., Ph.D.

Phone   212/854-4646
Fax   212/932-0602

Columbia offers a traditional history program with courses addressing a wide variety of topics. *Course Highlights: Decolonization of South Asia; Research Seminar on African History; Problematics in International Relations.*

✦ *Key Faculty*

Eric Foner: Civil war and reconstruction; slavery; 19th century U.S. history.
Admissions Information: Graduate School of Arts and Sciences; 107 Low Memorial Library; New York, NY 10027; Phone 212/854-4737; Fax 212/854-2863.

Princeton University   History

Princeton University
Department of History
Princeton, NJ 08544

Degree: Ph.D.

Phone   609/258-5529

Princeton offers a wide variety of courses, giving students the opportunity to draw on many topics to create a degree that suits their needs. *Course Highlights: Modern African History; Race and Politics in the U.S., 1820–1900; Topics in the History of Sex and Gender; Modern Chinese History.*

✦ *Key Faculty*

Natalie Davis: Social history; women's history.
Admissions Information: Princeton University; Admissions Office; 307 Nassau Hall; Princeton, NJ 08544; Phone 609/258-3034.

University of California, Berkeley

History

Department of History
3229 Dwinelle Hall #2550
University of California
Berkeley, CA 94720-2550

Degrees: B.A., M.A., Ph.D.

Phone   510/642-1971
Fax   510/643-5323

The UC Berkeley History program offers both traditional and non-traditional courses. *Course Highlights: Modern Contemporary Jewish Thought; Migration Within and Immigration to the U.S.; Latin American History; The Modern Middle East.*

✦ *Key Faculty*

Leon Litwack: Black history; labor history; race relations.
Admissions: (Address as above); Phone 510/642-2378.

OTHER PROGRAMS

San Francisco State University
Department of History
1600 Holloway Avenue
San Francisco, CA 94132
✦ *Key Faculty:* **Abdiel Onate**

Degrees: B.A., M.A.

Phone   415/338-1604

Human Rights

University of London

University of London
Institute of Commonwealth Studies
Russell Square
London WC1B 5DS

Understanding & Securing Human Rights

Degree: M.A.

Phone   +44 171 580 5876
Fax   +44 171 255 2610

The degree consists of three courses and a dissertation of 10-15,000 words. The dissertation is divided into three papers, each with two parts:

Paper 1 will acquaint students with the history of legal and political systems; the international system; various declarations, covenants, and bills of rights; and the human rights movement. It will also expose them to various philosophical perspectives on rights. It will consider definitions of human rights and their implications from the perspective of academic lawyers, philosophers, and social scientists.

Paper 2 will consist mainly of presentation by human rights professionals, which will acquaint students with the practical difficulties that confront them and the strategies and techniques that can be used to cope with those difficulties.

Paper 3 will integrate the work done in Papers 1 and 2 by examining issues and case studies that require students to link the perspectives of historians, philosophers, academic lawyers, and social scientists in Paper 1 with the analysis of practicalities in Paper 2.

✦ *Key Faculty*

James Manor: Director, Institute of Commonwealth Studies; commonwealth politics.
Elizabeth Nissan: Anthropology; former head of Asia research at Amnesty International.
Admissions Information: (Address as above).

Although no university in the U.S. offers an undergraduate or masters degree in Human Rights, there are several universities that offer the opportunity to create a human rights focus within another discipline. What follows is basic contact information on some interesting programs, so that you may request information and make your own assessments.

American University   Degree: L.L.M
Law degree with emphasis on human rights   Phone   202/885-2612
✦ *Key Faculty:* **Robert Goldman**

Columbia University   Degree: L.L.M.
Human Rights Program within the Law School Phone   212/854-2640
✦ *Key Faculty:* **Paul Martin**

Harvard University   Degree: L.L.M.
Harvard Law School   Phone   617/495-9362
Contact: **Jenny Green**

Harvard University   Degrees: M.P.H., M.S.
Harvard School of Public Health   Phone   617/496-4370
Courses can be taken in the Francois Xavier
Bagnould School of Health and Human Rights

SUNY-Buffalo   Degree: J.D.
School of Law   Phone   716/645-2060
✦ *Key Faculty:* **Virginia Leary**

University of California, Berkeley   Phone   510/642-0965
Human Rights Program
Townsend Center
✦ *Key Faculty:* **Rita Maran**

University of Denver   Degrees: B.A., M.A., Ph.D.
School of International Studies   Phone   303/871-2563
✦ *Key Faculty:* **Jack Donnelly**

Law

City University of New York   Law

City University of New York
School of Law
65-21 Main Street
Flushing, NY 11367

Degree: J.D.

Phone   718/575-4200
Fax   718/575-4275

CUNY School of Law is a public law school with a curriculum that emphasizes the importance of serving the public interest. Students look at such issues as the law's response to interactions between bureaucracies and ordinary people, the treatment of minorities, the desire for democratic participation in administrative decision making, and alternatives to adversary litigation. Clinics include the Immigrants' Rights Clinic, the Defender Clinic, the Battered Women's Rights Clinic, and the International Women's Human Rights Clinic. Many students elect a concentration and are placed in New York law offices two days a week. There is a low ratio of students to teachers and a significant emphasis on clinical work. *Course Highlights: Poverty Law in the U.S.: Legal Strategies for the 1990s; Sexuality and the Law; AIDS and the Law.*

Admissions Information: Admissions Office; (Address as above).

Harvard University   Law

Harvard Law School
Cambridge, MA 02138

Degrees: J.D. & joint programs
Phone   617/495-3100

In addition to the J.D. degree, Harvard Law School offers the Program on Negotiation, which is dedicated to improving the process of reaching agreements among individuals, organizations, and nations. Drawing upon specialists in all fields, the program is comprised of a consortium of professors from the greater Boston area. Seminars focus on such topics as public policy disputes, community conflict, international negotiations, culture and gender issues in negotiations, and environmental disputes. For more information, write: Program on Negotiation; Harvard Law School; 500 Pound Hall; Cambridge, MA 02138.

Harvard Law School also offers a Human Rights Program. Students have opportunities for documentary and field research and internships with non-governmental and human rights organizations. The program also has a visiting speakers series and hosts international conferences and retreats on human rights. *Course Highlights: Human Rights and International Law; Immigration Law.*

✦ Key Faculty

Gary Bellow: Movement to establish community legal services and legal clinics (one of the founders); community-based advocacy with poor women; lawyering for poor people.
Alan Dershowitz: Civil liberties; First Amendment issues.
Frank Sander: Mediation; alternative dispute resolution.
Admissions Information: Harvard Law School; Admissions Office; 1563 Massachusetts Avenue; Cambridge, MA 02138.

------◆------

New College of California   Law

New College of California   **Degree: J.D.**
School of Law
50 Fell Street   **Phone   415/241-1300**
San Francisco, CA 94102   **Fax   415/861-7566**

New College School of Law was founded in 1973 at the vortex of the public-interest law movement inspired by the struggles for social justice that characterized the 1960s. The program seeks to combine both theory and practice by offering students various courses, skills training seminars, on-campus clinical programs, and on the job training. The Housing Advocacy Clinic places students with a professor at the San Francisco Neighborhood Legal Assistance Foundation office to offer direct representation and intake services to low-income clients facing evictions. *Course Highlights: Federal Civil Rights Litigation; Labor and Employment Law; Domestic Relations.*

✦ Key Faculty

Chris Kanios: Represented organized maritime and sugar workers and plaintiffs; Board of Directors, Street Law Project and Swords to Plowshares.
Admissions Information: Admissions Office; (Address as above); Phone 415/241-1353.

New York University   Law

New York University
School of Law
Graduate Admissions
PO Box 904
New York, NY 10276-0904

Degree: J.D.

Phone   212/998-6060

NYU believes in the importance of educating students for public service careers, offering multiple scholarships for students pursuing public service and other traditionally low-paying legal jobs. NYU also offers special programs on Civil Liberties and Human Rights as well as clinical programs in Civil Rights, Environmental Law, International Human Rights, Juvenile Rights, Urban Law, International Environmental Law, and Civil Litigation. *Course Highlights: Humanitarian Principles and Armed Conflict; Human Rights in the Third World; Women and the Law.*

Admissions Information: (Address as above).

Northeastern University   Law

Northeastern University
School of Law
400 Huntington Avenue
Boston, MA 02115

Degree: J.D.

Phone   617/373-2395
Fax   617/373-8865

Northeastern University School of Law places a great emphasis on public interest. More than 20 percent of the school's graduates work in public interest settings. Northeastern also offers the only cooperative ("co-op") legal education program in the nation. Students complete a traditional first year of academic study; thereafter, they alternate every three months between academic study and co-ops in the legal workplace. There are more than 750 co-op employers nationwide and, on average, 35 percent of students secure post-graduate positions with their former co-op employers. *Course Highlights: Welfare Law; Employment Discrimination; Health Law.*

Admissions Information: (Address as above).

Stanford University   Law

Office of Admissions
Stanford Law School
Stanford, CA 94305-8610

Degrees: J.D., J.S.D., M.L.S., J.S.M., J.D./M.B.A.
Phone   415/723-2465
Fax   415/725-0253

Stanford Law School offers many special programs including Environmental and Natural Resources Law; Negotiation, Litigation, Alternative Methods of Dispute Resolution; Public Interest and Government Practice; and Public Policy. The school sponsors clinical programs on such issues as domestic violence, immigration, civil rights, disability rights, housing, and welfare law. Most clinical training with clients takes place at the East Palo Alto Community Law Project. *Course Highlights: Immigration Law and Policy; Environmental Law and Processes; Gender, Law, and Public Policy.*

✦ Key Faculty

Barbara Babcock: Criminal law.
Bill Hing: Immigration; lawyering process for social change; race relations.
Gerald Lopez: Civil rights litigation; self-help and lay lawyering; community practice; subordination.
William Simon: Business associations; legal profession; employment.
Kim Taylor: Criminal defense; subordinated communities.
Admissions Information: (Address as above).

Whittier Law School   Children's Rights

Advancement Office
Whittier Law School
5353 West Third Street
Los Angeles, CA 90020

Degree: J.D.

Phone   213/938-3621 x143
Fax   213/938-3460

The Whittier Law School Center for Children's Rights was founded in response to one of the most pressing problems of our time—the plight of economically powerless children thrust into our legal system. Committed to meeting the need for trained children's advocates, Whittier believes that attorneys should develop skills in law school appropriate for this role. To this end, the law school provides a maximum of 25 entering students the opportunity to become Children's Fellows and train for a future as children's advocates.

Concurrent with the traditional three-year Juris Doctor program, the Children's Rights Center curriculum was developed on the theory that advocates for children's rights are best trained in a small program setting. The interdisciplinary approach combines classroom and clinical components that allow students to participate in specialized legal writing classes, multi-disciplinary seminars, and independent study projects.

Fellows are placed in externships that focus primarily on children's issues. Fellows may clerk for Superior Court Judges in the Child Dependency Courts and Juvenile Delinquency Courts, litigate cases in the Office of the District Attorney and County Counsel, or assist the Public Defender in representing allegedly delinquent youth. There are additional externship possibilities with legal aid offices. *Course Highlights: Juvenile Justice; Children's Rights Seminar.*

✦ *Key Faculty*

Judith Daar: Bioethics (surrogate parenting, consent for children's health care, children and AIDS); legal process; real property; wills; trusts.
William Patton: Former Deputy State Public Defender specializing in juvenile defense in the California Courts of Appeal and the Supreme Court; child abuse and neglect.
Admissions Information: (Address as above).

Yale University   Law

Yale Law School
PO Box 208329
New Haven, CT 06520-8329

Degrees: M.S.L., J.D., LL.M., J.S.D.
Phone   203/432-4992
Fax   203/432-2592

Established at Yale Law School in 1989, the Orville H. Schell, Jr. Center for International Human Rights is an interdisciplinary research organization that provides an intellectual framework to meet the concerns of human rights advocates. It looks at the long-term theoretical issues within Human Rights while also providing a dialogue between intellectuals and human rights advocates. In the past, the Center has sponsored talks on the right to shelter, redefining national security, human rights and labor rights, war crimes and genocide.

Also within Yale Law School are several clinical programs. The Environmental Protection Clinic addresses environmental law and policy problems for environmental groups, government agencies, and international bodies. The Lowenstein International Human Rights Law Clinic helps human rights organizations and individual victims of human rights violations. The Nonprofit Organizations Clinic provides legal assistance to non-profit organizations that cannot afford to hire a private lawyer.

Admissions Information: (Address as above).

Peace Studies

Antioch University

The McGregor School
of Antioch University
800 Livermore Street
Yellow Springs, OH 45387

Conflict Resolution/ International Relations/ Peace Studies

Degrees: B.A., M.A.

Phone   513/767-6321
Fax   513/767-6461

The Peace Studies program at Antioch University looks at both negative and positive peace, direct and indirect forms of structural violence, and multi-disciplinary peace theories that consider interpersonal, intergroup, and international relations. Co-op, study abroad and second language components are additional resources. The Peace Studies program also encourages students to pursue and develop their own particular interest within the major. *Undergraduate Course Highlights: Global Peace Movements in the Information Age; Prospects for Peace in the 21st Century: Alternative Futures.*

The Master of Arts program in Conflict Resolution is built on four basic components. Core Sessions are three-week, on-campus sessions focused on theoretical development and practice skills. Individually Designed Learning allows students to focus their education programs in areas of particular interests. Practicum gives students an opportunity to broaden their experiences in conflict resolution through a field placement. A thesis is required, based on the student's learning throughout the program. Antioch houses the Headquarters of the International Peace Research Association (IPRA), an association of peace researchers and educators from more than 70 countries. *Graduate Course Highlights: Intercultural and Gender Issues in Conflict Resolution; Peace, Justice and Ethical Issues in Conflict Resolution.*

✦ Key Faculty

Paul Smoker: International project to reconceptualize security including political, social economic, ecological, cultural and technological dimensions; increasing global effectiveness of global peace movements.
Admissions Information: Office of Admissions; (Address as above); Phone 513/767-6325.

Brandeis University

Peace & Conflict Studies

Brandeis University
Peace and Conflict Studies
Department of Sociology
Waltham, MA 02254-9110

Degree: B.A.—6 course program
with a traditional major
Phone 617/736-2642
Fax   617/736-2653

The Peace Studies program examines the arms race and the threat of nuclear conflagration. With the end of the Cold War and the reduction of the nuclear threat, the focus is now on conflicts and non-violent ways to manage and resolve them. Students are required to take either *Causes and Prevention of War*, or *War and Possibilities of Peace*, and a minimum of five other courses divided into five areas: Violence and War, Explaining Conflict: Global Political and Economic Dimensions, Explaining Conflict: Resource Dimensions, Explaining Conflict: Social and Cultural Dimensions, and Conflict Management and Peace-Building. *Course Highlights: Managing Ethnic Conflict; Inequality and Social Identity; Population and Poverty in the Third World.*

✦ *Key Faculty*

Gordon Fellman: War and peace; empowerment; Marx; Freud; social class; equality; Israeli-Palestinian confrontation.

Cornell University

Peace Studies

Cornell University
Peace Studies Program
130 Uris Hall
Ithaca, NY 14853-7601

Degrees: Certificate with another degree
(B.A., M.A.)
Phone 607/255-6484
Fax   607/254-5000
E-mail eds3@cornell.edu

The Peace Studies program is not a separate degree-granting body. Rather, it is intended to stimulate teaching and research in the prevention and moderation of war through any relevant department at Cornell, for example: Government, Economics, History, or Sociology. Graduate students seeking to work within the Peace Studies program must first be admitted to the graduate program of one of Cornell's traditional academic fields.

The Peace Studies program is an interdisciplinary program devoted to research and teaching on the problems of war and peace, arms control and disarmament, and collective violence. The program also supports projects on ethnicity and international conflict, global environmental change and social justice, economic conversion of the defense industry, and women in the military. *Course Highlights: Non-Proliferation After the Cold War; The North-South Global Divide; The Language and Literature of Political Violence.*

✦ *Key Faculty*

Judith Reppy: War and peace in the nuclear age; military; technology.

Earlham School of Religion   Peace & Justice Studies

Earlham School of Religion
Peace and Justice Studies
228 College Avenue
Richmond, IN 47374

Degree: M.A.
Phone   317/983-1423 or
              800/432-1377
Fax   317/983-1688

The Earlham School of Religion offers an M.A. in Religion with an emphasis in Peace and Justice Studies as well as a Master of Ministry/Divinity with a specialization in Peace and Justice Studies. The two Master's programs combine religious studies with peace and justice concerns. As a Quaker seminary, the school provides an open, ecumenical community exploring social justice issues in the tradition of the Religious Society of Friends. *Course Highlights: Spirituality for Peace and Justice; Religious Responses to War and Violence; Liberation Theology.*

✦ *Key Faculty*

Anthony Bing: Director; English; Middle East conflict; Intifada.
Admissions Information: (Address as above).

Five College Program   Peace and World Security Studies (PAWSS)

Five College Program in Peace
    and World Security Studies
Box SS
Hampshire College
Amherst, MA 01002

Degrees: Academic Enrichment Program

Phone   413/549-4600
Fax   413/582-5620

Although the PAWSS program does not offer a formal concentration in the field, interested students are encouraged to integrate a number of the courses into their existing program of study, or to design their own concentration. Students may choose from a wide range of courses at the five colleges participating in the program: Amherst College, Hampshire College, Mount Holyoke College, Smith College, and the University of Massachusetts at Amherst. Students interested in peace and world security affairs take classes from the following areas: War and Peace; Ethnicity, Nationalism, and Political Violence; Mediation and Conflict Resolution; Development, Human Rights, and Social Change; International Relations and Foreign Policy; or International Law and Organizations. *Course Highlights: War, Revolution, and Peace; Alternatives to the Adversary Process; Peasant Revolution and Village in Modern China.*

✦ *Key Faculty*

Michael Klare: International peace; security affairs.

George Mason University   Conflict Analysis & Resolution

George Mason University
Institute for Conflict Analysis and Resolution
4400 University Drive
Fairfax, VA 22030-4444

Degrees: M.S., Ph.D.

Phone   703/993-1300
Fax   703/993-1302

The Institute for Conflict Analysis and Resolution offers both a M.S. and a Ph.D. Both programs are taught with the mission of advancing the understanding and resolution of significant and persistent human conflicts among individuals, small groups, communities, ethnic groups, and nations.

Established in 1982, the Master's program is a two-year program emphasizing theory development, research methods, and professional practice. Students examine negotiation, mediation, and problem solving, implementing this knowledge in a required internship. *Course Highlights: Ethnic and Cultural Factors in Conflict; Third Party Roles, Resources, and Ethics; Integration of Theory and Practice.*

The Doctoral program provides advanced training in the theory of conflict and conflict resolution. Students are trained for a variety of professions including researchers, theoreticians, and teachers in higher education. The Doctoral program stresses background in a substantive area of conflict, familiarity with current processes of conflict resolution, and knowledge of theory, research, conflict resolution methods and their interrelationships. *Course Highlights: Mind and Conflict; Theory Development.*

✦ *Key Faculty*

Juliana Birkhoff: Theory Coordinator, Applied Practice and Theory Program of the Institute and Clinical Faculty; economic and racial roots of conflict in urban areas.
Frank Blechman: Public policy disputes; education in schools.
Admissions Information: Office of Admissions; George Mason University; Fairfax, VA 22030-4444.

Juniata College   Peace & Conflict Studies

Juniata College   Degrees: B.A., B.S.
Peace and Conflict Studies   Phone   814/643-4310
Huntingdon, PA 16652   Fax   814/643-6034

The program examines the causes and consequences of violence and conflict across all levels of human interaction, interpersonal to international. It includes the study of warfare, the analysis of the causes and consequences of violence, the exploration of issues involved in limiting or preventing conflict and violence, and in creating structures that enhance justice. The program also explores the methods used for waging conflicts and settling, managing, and resolving them.

The program encourages students to study abroad and/or to spend a semester in an internship related to their academic interests. The program at Juniata is interdisciplinary and there are many opportunities for students to pursue individualized programs of study that combine areas of interest, for example: peace and the environment, gender and conflict, or the anthropology of war. *Course Highlights: Gender and Conflict; Nonviolence; The Idea of War.*

✦ *Key Faculty*

Celia Cook-Huffman: Chair, Peace and Conflict Studies Committee at the Baker Institute of Peace and Conflict Studies; conflict resolution; violence; gender.
Taylor Highlands: Director, Baker Institute for Peace and Conflict Studies; peace studies; religion; India.

Admissions Information: Juniata College; Office of Admission; 1700 Moore Street; Huntingdon, PA 16652-2119.

Manchester College

Manchester College
Peace Studies Institute and
Program in Conflict Resolution
North Manchester, IN 46962

Conflict Resolution

Degrees: A.A., B.A., B.S. Peace Studies
Phone   219/982-5343
Fax   219/982-6868
E-mail klbrown@manchester.edu (Internet)
         kbrown@igc.org (Peacenet)

Manchester College hosts the oldest academic peace studies program in the United States, offering concentrations in interpersonal and intergroup, global and international peacemaking, and philosophical and theological bases for peacemaking. Individually designed concentrations are encouraged, as are all majors encompassing a traditional field. Study abroad during the junior year is encouraged. January interim study-travel courses, practicums, and internships are offered regularly. Manchester also offers a concentration in gender studies, and an interdisciplinary major in environmental studies. *Course Highlights: Religions and War; International Law and Organization; Civilization of South Asia.*

✦ *Key Faculty*

Ken Brown: Non-violence.
Admissions Information: Admissions Center; Manhattan College; Riverdale, NY 10471-4098.

Manhattan College

Peace Studies Program
433 Manhattan Hall
Manhattan College
Bronx, NY 10471

Peace Studies

Degree: B.A.

Phone   718/920-0305
Fax   718/920-0995

Challenged by the problems of regional and nuclear war, the civil rights movement, and economic injustice, the students and faculty of Manhattan College initiated the B.A. in Peace Studies in 1968. The program is dedicated to the academic and moral search for solutions to the problems of war and human injustice. The program examines five areas: war, social justice, conflict resolution, nonviolent strategies, and world community. In addition to course work, an internship is required. Previous Peace Studies internships have included the United Nations, Pax Christi, Educators of Social Responsibility, and ABC News. *Course Highlights: Media Criticism; Literature of the Developing World; The Anatomy of Peace.*

✦ **Key Faculty**

Joseph Fahey: Religious studies; peace studies.

Syracuse University	Analysis & Resolution of Conflicts

Syracuse University
Program on the Analysis and
Resolution of Conflicts (PARC)
410 Maxwell Hall
Syracuse, NY 13244

Degrees: B.A., M.A., Ph.D.

Phone   315/443-2367
Fax   315/443-3818
E-mail   rar@mailbox.syr.edu

PARC is an interdisciplinary center within Syracuse University's Maxwell School of Citizenship and Public Affairs. Established in 1986, the program is dedicated to enhancing knowledge about social conflicts (their nature, course of development, and possible resolution) through theory building, research, education, and practice.

PARC conducts its work through the efforts of its approximately 65 faculty associates and nearly 100 affiliated graduate students. Faculty and graduate students come from all social science disciplines and work within a structure that encourages cross disciplinary collaboration and innovation. PARC offers certificates in conflict resolution, international peace studies, and environmental conflict resolution. *Course Highlights: National Defense: Military, Economic, and Cultural; Environmental Ideas; Social Role of the Non-Conformists.*

✦ **Key Faculty**

Robert Rubinstein: Political and medical anthropology; cross-cultural negotiation; international security and conflict resolution; international health and development.

Tufts University   Peace & Justice Studies

Tufts University
Peace and Justice Studies Program
109 Easton Hall
Medford, MA 02155

Degree: Undergrad Certificate
Phone   617/628-5000 x2261
Fax   617/627-3032
E-mail dbryan@pearl.tufts.edu

Peace and Justice Studies (PJS) program provides an interdisciplinary structure for examining the obstacles, conditions, and paths to achieving a just global peace. Two central areas are emphasized: first, the study of the causes of war, the techniques of war prevention, and the conditions and structures of a just peace; and second, the origins, strategies, and visions of social movements seeking social justice and ecological sustainability. PJS encourages students to explore their education through peace and feminist pedagogies, and requires experiential learning through internships and community service. The annual Institute in Social Movements and Strategic Nonviolence, a summer internship-seminar project, is open to all undergraduate or graduate students. *Course Highlights: Racial and Ethnic Minorities; Race, Gender, Class, and Sexuality; The American Sixties.*

✦ Key Faculty

Paul Joseph: Peace politics; peace cultures in comparative perspective.
Kathleen Weiler: Women teachers; feminist education and pedagogy.
Gerald Gill: African American pacifism; conscientious objection; resistance to militarism; comparative history of civil rights movement efforts across the U.S.
Dale Bryan: Design of internships and experiential learning practices in nonviolent social movements; impact of peace pedagogy for developing nonviolent consciousness and collective identity.

University of California, Berkeley   Peace & Conflict Studies

Peace and Conflict Studies
361 Campbell Hall
University of California
Berkeley, CA 94720

Degrees: B.A. and Minor

Phone   510/643-6465
Fax   510/642-4607

Founded in 1983, the Peace and Conflict Studies program focuses on the study of peace, conflict, and a just world order. The program provides systematic and interdisciplinary analyses of confrontation and cooperation among individuals, groups, and nations. Courses explore the social, psychological, economic, political, and ecological dimensions of conflict and peace from a global and integrative perspective. Because the major is interdisciplinary, students choose a field of interest and take classes from other departments that focus on their area of concentration. Students are required to take one class from each of the following five areas: Peace, War, and Global Systems; Ethics, Culture, and Power; Conflict Analysis, Social Change, and Nonviolent Resolution; Political Economy and Resource Distribution; and Environment, Population, and Migration. *Course Highlights: Conflict Resolution: Theory and Practice; Human Rights; Nonviolence.*

✦ Key Faculty

Jerry Sanders: Global change and world order; international conflict and conflict resolution; war and culture.

Admissions Information: Office of Undergraduate Admissions; University of California; Berkeley, CA 94720.

University of Colorado

Social Conflict Concentration Coordinator
Department of Sociology
Campus Box 327
University of Colorado
Boulder, CO 80309-0327

Social Conflict

Degrees: B.A., M.A., Ph.D.

Phone   303/492-2623 or 6427
Fax   303/492-8878

The Department of Sociology has recast its Social Conflict Concentration as a conflict and change specialization within the department. Seven full-time faculty regularly offer graduate seminars in social movements, conflict management, conflict theory (negotiation and mediation), nonviolence, peace and war, and modern Marxist theory, as well as a practicum in conflict management. All of the faculty mentor M.A. and Ph.D. students in conflict- and change-related research. There are undergraduate counterpart conflict and change courses in the sociology curriculum that graduate assistants may offer for teaching experience. The Conflict Research Consortium and the Center for the Study of Violence, both nationally-recognized programs affiliated with the department, provide research and practice opportunities for graduate students. *Course Highlights: Social Stratification; Sociology of War; Collective Action.*

+ *Key Faculty*

Thomas Mayer: Analysis of revolutions; war and arms races; mathematical models in conflict analysis.

Paul Wehr: Conflict resolution theory and method; nonviolent collective action; environmental sociology.

University of Denver   International Studies

International Studies   Degrees: B.A., M.A., Ph.D.
University of Denver
Ben M. Cherrington Hall Room 102   Phone   800/525-9495
Denver, CO 80208   Fax   303/871-2456

Undergraduate study in international relations begins with a foundation in international politics, comparative politics, and international economics. It progresses with immersion into the language, history, economics, politics, and culture of specific geographic regions (Latin America, Asia, the Middle East, Africa, or Europe). Students choose a cluster of elective courses that concentrate on a particular interest like issues of war and peace including the causes of war, traditional conflict in the Middle East, and arms races. Study will culminate in an advanced research project.

The M.A. and Ph.D. in International Studies include concentrations in global conflict, human rights, international economics, policy analysis, international politics, and other relevant fields. The Graduate School of International Studies (GSIS) is one of only 15 in the country to hold membership in the prestigious Association of Professional Schools of International Affairs (APSIA) and has been recognized by the U.S. Department of Education as a National Resource Center for the study of cooperation and conflict in the post-Cold War world. The GSIS also publishes *Africa Today* and *The Monograph Series in World Affairs. Course Highlights: Ethics and Development; Outbreak of War; Human Rights and American Foreign Policy.*

+ *Key Faculty*

Thomas Rowe: Dean, International Studies; Member, North American Trade Dispute Resolution Committee; international organization; human rights; conflict; international politics.

Admissions Information: Office of Admission; University of Denver; 2199 South University Blvd.; Denver, CO 80208; Phone 800/525-9495.

University of North Dakota   Peace Studies

Center for Peace Studies
University of North Dakota
PO Box 7102
Grand Forks, ND 58202-7102

Degrees: B.A. and Minor

Phone   701/777-3250

Peace Studies is an interdisciplinary program that draws its faculty from various departments such as law, medicine, philosophy, economics, religious studies, anthropology, sociology, and political science. The program has two main goals: to encourage critical scholarly development among students and faculty about the comparatively unexamined history and contemporary literature of peace, war, and social justice; to offer students opportunities for educational and professional enrichment, as well as active democratic citizenship on issues related to peace and social justice, grassroots organizing, public and international service, and conflict resolution and negotiation. *Course Highlights: Moral Thought in a Nuclear Age; Social Change; World Food Patterns.*

✦ *Key Faculty*

Kristin Sorenson: Feminist theory; human rights; conflict analysis; nonviolent social change; politics of language.
Admissions Information: Office of Enrollment Services; Box 8135; University of North Dakota; Grand Forks, ND 58202; Phone 701/777-4463.

University of Notre Dame   Peace Studies

University of Notre Dame
Kroc Institute for International Peace Studies
Hesburgh Center
PO Box 639
Notre Dame, IN 46556

Degrees: M.A.; concentration at
     B.A. and Ph.D. level with
     other course of study
Phone   219/631-6970
Fax   219/631-6973

The Institute for International Peace Studies (IIPS) offers an M.A. in Peace Studies with four concentrations designed for different vocational paths: International Peace and World Order for students seeking to become international civil servants, national security experts, or diplomats; Cultural, Philosophical, and Religious Dimensions of Peace and Justice for those interested in church-related administration and education; Conflict Resolution and Dispute Settlement for civil rights activists and labor relations specialists; and Social Change for Peace for potential leaders in international voluntary organizations, political activists, and lobbyists. *Course Highlights: Gross Human Rights Violations; Community, Identity, and Nationalism; Crosscultural Encounters.*

Students interested in studying Peace on the undergraduate level may complement their major field with the Concentration in Peace Studies (CPS). This 15-credit-hour multidisciplinary program focuses on issues of peace, violence, justice, and human rights. *Course Highlights: Ethics of Development; Nonviolent Social Change; International Migration.*

Students within the Ph.D. program of the university's Departments of Government and International Studies, Economics, Sociology, or Theology can work with Institute fellows and focus on issues of peace and world order as a sub field of their Ph.D. program.

✦ Key Faculty

Robert Johansen: Senior Fellow and Director of Graduate Studies, Kroc Institute; former President, World Policy Institute; founding editor-in-chief, *World Policy Journal;* government; international studies.
Admissions Information: (Address as above).

University of San Francisco   Peace & Justice Studies

University of San Francisco
Peace and Justice Studies Program
Department of Politics
2130 Fulton Street
San Francisco, CA 94117

Degree: Certificate in Peace and
Justice Studies can be
completed to complement any
B.A. degree.
Phone   415/666-6349
Fax   415/666-2346

The program emphasizes the following themes: peace, war, and conflict; human rights, repression, and violence; economic justice, ecology, and development; and social movements and change. The program is based in the Politics Department but draws on courses from other social sciences and humanities, as well as from the Women's Studies and Legal Studies programs. Peace Studies offers an internship program based on its Fieldwork Directory of 400 Bay Area peace and human rights organizations. The program recently hosted the Peace Studies Association Annual Conference. The program houses and edits *Peace Review* (Robert Elias, Editor; Jennifer Turpin, Senior Editor), a transnational quarterly distributed in more than 40 nations. *Course Highlights: Human Rights and Global Change; Women, Men, and Violence; The Politics of American Justice.*

✦ Key Faculty

Robert Elias: Human rights; alternative development; violence (including criminal violence); the media.
Jennifer Turpin: Violence; women's studies; Russian studies.

University of St. Thomas

University of St. Thomas
Justice and Peace Studies
Mail #4137
2115 Summit Avenue
St. Paul, MN 55105-1096

Justice & Peace Studies

Degree: B.A. Major and Minor
Phone 612/962-5325
Fax   612/962-6110 — Attn:
       Friar David Smith
E-mail dwsmith@stthomas.edu (Internet)
       dwsmith@igc.apc.org (Peacenet)

Justice and Peace studies is an interdisciplinary program designed to prepare students to be responsible critics of contemporary societies and effective agents for positive social transformation. The program makes use of four stages: experience of poverty and injustice, descriptive analysis, (economic, political, and social realities of a culture and the historical events that produced them), normative analysis (moral values, alternative possibilities), and action possibilities (strategies and skills). The ten-course major (nine for a double major) requires five core courses: Introduction to Justice and Peace Studies; Theologies of Justice, Peace, Prosperity, and Security; Active Nonviolence; Conflict Resolution; and Methods and Resources. An internship is also required. The program is strongly interdisciplinary and interfaith. It promotes understanding and appreciation of widely diverse ideologies, cultures, and world views. Special attention is given to Roman Catholic social teaching in the context of pluralistic world societies.

✦ Key Faculty

David Smith: Implications for justice and peace of Christian Scriptures; major global religious and non-religious world views.

Political Science

Boston University

Political Science

Department of Political Science
Boston University
232 Bay State Road
Boston, MA 02215

Degrees: B.A., Ph.D.

Phone   617/353-2540
Fax   617/353-5508

The faculty in the Political Science Department represent a wide range of ideologies and outlooks, which are reflected in their teaching. The professors mentioned below are among the more progressive faculty, and their classes may focus on aspects of social change. *Course Highlights: Comparative Politics of the Middle East; The Legislative Process; Politics and the Media.*

✦ *Key Faculty*

Betty Zisk: Interest groups; the media; social movements.
Irene Grendzier: Middle East.
Graduate Admissions Information: Graduate Admissions; Boston University; 725 Commonwealth Avenue; Boston, MA 02215; Phone 617/353-2693.
Undergraduate Admissions Information: Undergraduate Admissions; Boston University; 881 Commonwealth Avenue; Boston, MA 02215; Phone 617/353-9770.

New School for Social Research

Political Science

New School for Social Research
Department of Political Science
65 Fifth Avenue
New York, NY 10003

Degrees: B.A., M.A., Ph.D.

Phone   212/229-5747
Fax   212/229-5315

The New School was founded as a forum where students could freely research controversial issues and non-conventional topics. The political science program is organized into three broad fields for teaching purposes: Political Theory, Growth and Structure of the American Polity, and State and Society in Global Perspective. The program begins with the study of the historical and theoretical developments that formed the discipline. Students then progress to developing their own program, undertaking research that is useful, enlightening, and beneficial to society. *Course Highlights: Brazilian Politics; Urban Politics; Labor Movements in the Third World.*

✦ Key Faculty

Adamantia Pollis: Comparative politics and human rights; the human rights movement; ethnicity in the Balkans.
Admissions: (Address as above).

University of Notre Dame — Government

University of Notre Dame
Department of Government and International Studies
314 O'Shaughnessy Hall
Notre Dame, IN 46556

Degrees: B.A., Ph.D.

Phone 219/631-7312
Fax 219/631-4268

The department has a high profile in several areas, including political theory, Latin American politics, German politics, constitutional studies, international human rights, religion and politics, and peace studies. *Graduate Course Highlights: International Humanitarian Issues; International Relations of Latin America; Politics of Tropical and Southern Africa.*

✦ Key Faculty

Scott Mainwaring: Latin American politics.
Admissions Information: (Address as above).

Public Health/Nutrition

Columbia University

Teachers College
Program in Nutrition and Education
Columbia University
Box 137
525 W. 120th Street
New York, NY 10027

Nutrition and Education

Degrees: M.S., Ed.D. in Nutrition Education
or Public Health Nutrition

Phone   212/678-3950
Fax   212/678-3123

Part of the Division of Health Services, Sciences, and Education, the Master's program in Nutrition Education allows students to follow course work in one of several areas: nutrition in public health, nutrition education, and nutrition and exercise physiology. Programs are unique in their emphasis on world hunger, food policy, and nutrition education. The Nutrition Education Resources Project has developed an "Earth Friends" curriculum linking nutrition and environmental issues. The program aims to provide students the following: a thorough grounding in nutrition sciences and an ability to evaluate critically the literature; the facility for identifying and analyzing determinants of food selection and nutritional status among both individuals and populations; the ability to facilitate individuals and groups in adopting nutritionally desirable behaviors through application of the behavioral sciences; and some practice in promoting both political and social change in the arena of nutrition and health. Because of the breadth of its aims, the program has long admitted academically qualified students with undergraduate degrees in fields other than nutrition or the related sciences, so long as they can meet the science prerequisites. *Course Highlights: A Survey of Nutrition: Fads and Popular Fallacies; Nutritional Ecology; Nutrition and Behavior.*

✦ *Key Faculty*

Sharon Akabas: Nutrition education of the consumer; effects of exercise on metabolism; interaction of nutrition science and policy.
Isobel Contento: Coordinator; psychosocial determinants of food choice and eating behavior in children and adolescents; consumer decision-making processes with respect to food; training of nutrition educators.
Joan Gussow: Environmental impacts of various dietary patterns; impact of economics and technology on the present and future relationship between humans and the food system; implications for women of changes in the food supply.
Admissions Information: (Address as above).

Columbia University

Public Health Nutrition

Columbia University
Program in Public Health Nutrition
School of Public Health
100 Haven Avenue, III-4E & 4F
New York, NY 10032

Degrees: M.S., M.P.H., Dr.P.H.

Phone   212/740-6103

The Program in Public Health Nutrition is affiliated with the Columbia Teachers College Program in Nutrition and Education and shares some of the same faculty and courses. The public health nutrition group conducts, coordinates, and leads activities at the school that integrate basic and clinical nutrition research with applied research. The group translates these findings into health promotion and disease prevention interventions, strategies, and policies. The Program in Public Health Nutrition integrates academic programs at the Master's and Doctoral level in nutritional epidemiology, maternal and child health nutrition, environmental nutrition, and other combined disciplines. *Course Highlights: Food and Nutrition: A Public Health Perspective; Environmental Nutrition; Community Nutrition Programs.*

Admissions Information: School of Public Health; Office of Admissions; 600 West 168th Street; New York, NY 10032; Phone 212/305-3927.

Cornell University

International Nutrition

Cornell University
International Nutrition Program
Division of Nutritional Sciences
210 Savage Hall
Ithaca, NY 14853-6301

Degrees: M.S., Ph.D.
Phone   607/255-4419
Fax   607/255-2608
E-mail   intl_nutr_mailbox@
          cornell.edu

The causes of inadequate nutrition are many and complex, involving social, economic, and political issues. The International Nutrition Program trains individuals who are dedicated to eliminating hunger, malnutrition, and chronic disease. The faculty have experience in many parts of the world, and their expertise covers the spectrum from basic biology to population-based interventions and policy. Courses are offered in the political, economic, sociological, clinical, and public health dimensions of nutrition. Study in international nutrition begins with a solid basis in human nutrition, including biochemistry, physiology, and laboratory methods. In addition to taking courses that emphasize the biological aspects of nutrition, students are expected to include appropriate course work that recognizes the social, cultural, agricultural, economic, and public health policy impacts of nutrition, as well as analytical methods. *Course Highlights: Epidemiology of Nutrition; Nutrition Introduction in Communities, a Global Perspective; International Nutrition Problems, Policies, and Programs.*

✦ Key Faculty

Jere Haas: Program Co-Director; nutritional sciences; anthropology; environmental causes and functional consequences of malnutrition during pregnancy and growth in developing countries; nutritional status and body composition as they relate to human performance and productivity in undernourished populations.

Jean-Pierre Habicht: Program Co-Director; nutritional epidemiology; discovery and application of social and biological sciences to solving hunger and nutrition problems of the poorest through policies and policy instruments (e.g., programs); determinants and consequences of maternal and child malnutrition and information (e.g., scientific knowledge, monitoring, surveillance) for decision making.

Michael Latham: International nutrition focusing on nutritional problems of developing countries, especially protein-energy malnutrition, vitamin A deficiency, and anemia; determinants of infant feeding practices; relationship of parasitic infections to nutrition; effect of iron supplementation on growth and appetite.

Admissions Information: (Address as above).

Johns Hopkins University

Johns Hopkins University
Department of Health Policy
and Management
School of Hygiene and Public Health
615 North Wolfe Street
Baltimore, MD 21205

Health Policy and Management

Degrees: Sc.M., M.H.S., Sc.D., Dr.P.H.,
Ph.D.; (Div. Pub. Hlth. does
not offer M.H.S. or Ph.D.)

Phone   410/955-2488
Fax   410/955-0876

The Department of Health Policy and Management is concerned with the effective, efficient, and equitable use of societal resources for the purpose of improving and maintaining the health of populations. Faculty conduct research on priority health policy and management issues facing industrialized and newly industrialized nations, train researchers in the broad areas of health care and the health system, train students for leadership roles in the private and public health sectors, and contribute to the formulation and implementation of changes to improve health and the health system. The department pursues these objectives through a range of research, educational, and service activities. The department is organized into four academic divisions: Behavioral Sciences and Health Education, Health Finance and Management, Health Policy, and Public Health. Students applying to the department must apply through one of the four academic divisions. *Course Highlights: Socioeconomic Environment of Health; Ethical Issues in Public Health; Understanding and Preventing Violence.*

✦ *Key Faculty*

Vicente Navarro: Health and social policy; international health; health care policy.
Admissions Information: (Address as above); Phone 410/955-3543; Fax 410/955-0464; E-mail admiss@jhuhyg.sph.jhu.edu.

Loma Linda University

Health Promotion and Education/International Health

Program in Health Promotion and Education
School of Public Health
Loma Linda University
Nichol Hall, Rm. 1511
Loma Linda, CA 92350

Degree: M.P.H. in Health Promotion and Education

Phone 909/824-4575
Fax 909/824-4087

Program in International Health
Loma Linda University
Nichol Hall, Rm. 1318
Loma Linda, CA 92350

Degree: M.P.H. in International Health

Phone 909/824-4902
Fax 909/824-4087

The Program in Health Promotion and Education trains graduates to function as community health educators in a variety of settings, both public and private. They are academically prepared to design, implement, and evaluate health education interventions; organize health promotion efforts; and assist individuals and communities to better utilize techniques of health behavior change. Specific emphasis is placed on group process and participation in voluntary health behavior change. Students designate a specific content area in which to focus course work. These areas include: community health, dependency behaviors, drug and alcohol, gerontology, and maternal and child health. Licensed health professionals may select from two additional emphases: health promotion and school nursing credential. *Course Highlights: Principles of Environmental Health; Community Programs Laboratory; Alcohol and Drug Dependency.*

The Program in International Health emphasizes management and technical aspects of primary health care interventions. Both health care professionals and applicants with a social science background are accepted. Opportunity is provided for field experience in community development and health care services management and among underserved populations in the U.S. and in developing countries. Students receive a foundation in health care organization, manpower development, environmental health, infectious disease control, maternal and child health/population programs, and the sociocultural aspects of planned change. Areas of faculty interest and expertise include maternal and child health care, vaccine trials and immunization program development, refugee health, training, and program planning and evaluation. *Course Highlights: Global Environmental Health; Agriculture in Development; Integrated Community Development; HIV/AIDS: Implications for Public Health; Refugee Health.*

✦ **Key Faculty**

Gordon Buhler: International health.
Barbara Frye: International health; health promotion and education; maternal-child health.
Richard Hart: International health; health promotion and education.
Jayakaran Job: International health; epidemiology; biostatistics.
Admissions Information: School of Public Health; Office of Admissions and Academic Records; Loma Linda University; Loma Linda, CA 92350; Phone 909/824-4546; Toll free 800/854-5661.

Rutgers University

Department of Nutritional Sciences
Cook College-Thompson Hall
PO Box 231
New Brunswick, NJ 08903-0231

Department of Nutritional Sciences

Degree: M.S., Ph.D.

Phone   908/932-9379
Fax   908/932-6837

The department offers two degree options: basic nutrition and applied nutrition. The basic nutrition option focuses on biochemical, physiological, and molecular aspects of nutrition. The applied nutrition option provides advanced training for registered dietitians, or those planning to become dietitians or to work in nutrition-related fields. It provides training in nutrition education and counseling and in community and clinical nutrition, with emphasis on the clinical, behavioral, and social science aspects of nutrition. The Ph.D. is only available in the basic nutrition area. *Course Highlights: Nutritional Aspects of Disease; Community Nutrition; Nutrition: A Biochemical and Physiological Basis.*

✦ *Key Faculty*

Michael Hamm: Nutrition; sustainable agriculture; localized food supplies; community empowerment.
Admissions Information: (Address as above).

University of California, Berkeley

School of Public Health

School of Public Health-Nutrition
140 Warren Hall
University of California
Berkeley, CA 94720-7360

Degrees: M.P.H., Dr.P.H.

Phone   510/642-4252
Fax   510/643-6981

Public Health Nutrition emphasizes the application of nutrition knowledge and research to the improvement of the health of populations. Course work focuses on the role of nutrition for the maintenance of health and the prevention of disease. The curriculum is designed to provide proficiency in the assessment of nutritional status and related community needs, the critical analysis of nutritional problems and their causes, the design of appropriate interventions to improve the nutritional status of populations, the evaluation of programs and policies, and the design and execution of research to expand the frontier of knowledge in these areas. *Course Highlights: Ethnic and Cultural Diversity in Health Status and Behavior; International Nutrition; Public Health Aspects of Maternal and Child Nutrition; Health and Social Policy in Mexico and Latin America.*

✦ *Key Faculty*

Barbara Abrams: Maternal and child nutrition; nutritional epidemiology.

Zak Sabry: Nutrition policy, international nutrition; public health nutrition.
Gladys Block: Nutritional epidemiology; cancer epidemiology.
Admissions Information: Student Services and Admissions Office; School of Public Health; University of California; Berkeley, CA 94720-7360.

OTHER PROGRAMS

Tulane University   Degrees: M.P.H., Dr.P.H.
School of Public Health and Tropical Medicine   Phone   504/584-3655
Department of International Health and Development
1501 Canal Street, Suite 1300
New Orleans, LA 70112
✦ *Key Faculty:* **Jane Bertrand, William Bertrand, Mahmud Khan, Robert Magnani, Nancy Mock, Robert Franklin, Carl Kendall, Jennifer Strickler, and David Hotchkiss**

Sociology

Binghamton University

Sociology

Department of Sociology
State University of New York at Binghamton
PO Box 6000
Binghamton, NY 13902-6000

Degree: Ph.D.

Phone 607/777-2628
Fax 607/777-4197

The graduate program in sociology is made up of two distinct concentrations: World Historical Social Change and American and Comparative Studies. World Historical Social Change studies long-term, large-scale historical change as well as the ongoing process of social change. Students look at issues such as: peasants and proletarians; development and underdevelopment; and identity, violence, and empowerment. The concentration in American and Comparative Studies focuses primarily on class, gender, race, and work. This concentration maintains a strong relationship with the Institute for Research on Multiculturalism and International Labor. *Course Highlights: Economic Expansion, Social Change, and Class Formation in the Periphery; Nation-States, Sex, and Modernity.*

✦ Key Faculty

James Geschwender: Gender; Canada.
James Petras: Development; revolutionary movements and class analysis; Latin America; Caribbean.
Mark Selden: Revolutionary movements; socialist development; East Asia (China).
Immanuel Wallerstein: Africanist; founder of World-Systems analysis.
Admissions Information: Graduate School Admissions; Binghamton University; PO Box 6000, Binghamton, NY 13902-6000.

Boston College

Sociology

Department of Sociology
Boston College
Chestnut Hill, MA 02167

Degrees: M.A. Ph.D.

Phone 617/552-8000

The Master's and Doctoral programs provide a strong background in conceptual and analytical skills and training in a wide variety of applied substantive fields. An overall focus of the graduate programs is social economy social justice, with special emphasis on race, class, and gender. Other areas of specialization include: political sociology and social movements, social change in policy planning, criminology, deviance and social control, ethnic relations, social psychology, social stratification, religion and society, sociology of art and cultural studies, medical sociology, complex organizations, and social problems of the economy.

The graduate Department of Sociology offers three special programs. The M.B.A./Ph.D. program allows students to receive an M.B.A. and a Ph.D. in sociology at the same time. Students seeking an M.A. in teaching may receive a concentration in sociology by completing 18 credits in the Sociology Department. The requirement for the M.A. in American Studies with a concentration in Sociology is 30 credit hours, including 12 in the major field. For more information, contact the Departmental Advisor to the American Studies Program. *Course Highlights: Legal and Illegal Violence Against Women; Images and Power; Law and Society.*

✦ *Key Faculty*

Severyn Bruyn: Community development; social economy; culture; participant observation; sociological aspects of business; social economy.
Charles Derber: Social and political economy; class theory; economic democracy; anti war, civil rights, and workplace democracy efforts.
William Gamson: Director, Media Research and Action Project (MRAP); efforts of social movements to change society; role of mass media in the process of change.
Sharlene Hesse-Biber: Co-founder, Women's Studies Program; gender; work; demography; methods; women and health.
Eve Spangler: Work and inequality; occupational safety, particularly for women workers; gender studies; health care.
Other interesting faculty: David Karp, Stephen Pfohl, and Diane Vaughan.

Cornell University   Development Sociology

Cornell University
Department of Rural Sociology
133 Warren Hall
Ithaca, NY 14853-7801

Degrees: B.S., M.S., Ph.D.
Phone 607/255-3163
Fax 607/255-9984
E-mail dlb17@cornell.edu

The B.S. degree in rural sociology has three concentrations: development sociology provides an understanding of processes and policies that influence social and economic development in the Third World, the United States, and other developed countries; population, environment, and society develops an understanding of social economic, and ecological causes and consequences of population change and insights into the relationships between social structure and the biophysical world; and social data and policy analysis provides research and analytical skills that are especially well suited for public sector employment. *Course Highlights: American Indian Tribal Governments; Aging and Aging Policy in the 1990s.*

The Graduate Field of Development Sociology is organized around four concentrations: community and regional sociology; rural and environmental sociology; population and development; and state, economy, and society. The graduate training program emphasizes both domestic and international issues pertaining to social change, agriculture and rural development and the environment. Three university- and college-wide programs are based in the Department of Rural Sociology: the Population and Development Program; the Community and Rural Development Institute; and the Farming Alternatives Program. *Course Highlights: Environment and Society; Global Patterns of International Migration; Sustainable Agriculture and Development.*

✦ *Key Faculty*

Shelley Feldman: Social restructuring and the transformation of work in the U.S. and South Asia; household food production systems; agricultural sustainability in the upland regions of Southeast Asia.
Charles Geisler: Role of sociology in conservation biology, in local control controversies, and in social impact assessment.
Philip McMichael: World-economic developments, including agricultural and food systems, state and state system restructuring; Pacific rim.

Harvard University

Harvard University
Department of Sociology
William James Hall
Cambridge, MA 02138

Sociology

Degrees: B.A., Ph.D.

Phone   617/495-3812
Fax   617/496-5794

Harvard University offers a B.A. in sociology as well as a Ph.D. The graduate program in sociology focuses on preparing its students for scholarly and applied research as well as teaching positions. *Course Highlights: Poverty and the American Underclass; Gender and Culture in Middle Eastern and Islamic Societies.*

✦ Key Faculty

Theda Skocpol: U.S. politics and public policies; protest movements; roots of social change.

Admissions Information: Graduate School of Arts and Sciences; Admissions Office; Byerly Hall, Second Floor; 8 Garden Street; Cambridge, MA 02138.

Johns Hopkins University   Sociology

Department of Sociology	Degrees: B.A., M.A., Ph.D.
Johns Hopkins University	Phone 410/516-7626
Baltimore, MD 21218	Fax 410/516-7590

The Department of Sociology has two main foci: Comparative International Development—sociological issues in national development that cut across countries and world regions; and Institutions and Individuals—the study of how three central social institutions (work, school, and family) affect and are affected by individuals. Students within the undergraduate program may choose (but are not required) to focus their studies on one of these two concentrations. *Course Highlights: Gender and Development in the Americas; Rebellion and Revolution in the World System; Immigration and Ethnicity.*

The department's graduate program is oriented toward the training of Ph.D.s in sociology. The M.A. degree is granted to students successfully completing eight courses but is only granted as part of the doctoral training sequence. The department also has three special programs as areas of concentration: Comparative and International Development; Institutions and Individuals; and Medical Sociology. *Course Highlights: Labor in the World System; Seminar on the Family; Theories of Social Change and Evolution.*

✦ Key Faculty

Christopher Chase-Dunn: Urbanization; social stratification; world-systems analysis.

Alejandro Portes: Urbanization and national development; international labor migration; social stratification; Latin America.

Beverly Silver: Historical sociology; world-systems analysis; social movements; political sociology.

New School for Social Research

Sociology

Department of Sociology
New School for Social Research
66 West 12th Street
New York, NY 10011

Degrees: M.A., Ph.D.

Phone   212/229-5737
Fax   212/229-5315

Using a variety of contemporary approaches to interpretation and research, the Department of Sociology builds on the work of social thinkers such as Marx, de Tocqueville, Weber, Durkheim, Simmel, Mead, Goffman, Parsons, Habermas, and Foucault. The department maintains strong ties to European and American traditions of critical, historical, comparative, and theoretical sociology. Its program offers specialization in social thought, the study of urban communities, comparative and historical analysis of social change, the sociology of culture, and political sociology. *Course Highlights: The Sociology of Neighborhoods; Modernity and its Discontents; Ideological, Cultural, and Economic Context of Human Rights.*

Admissions Information: Graduate Faculty Admissions; New School for Social Research; 65 Fifth Avenue, Room 110; New York, NY 10003; Phone 800/523-5411.

University of California, Berkeley

Sociology

Department of Sociology
University of California
Berkeley, CA 94720

Degrees: B.A., M.A., Ph.D.

Phone   510/642-1657

The repute of Berkeley's Department of Sociology is a product of the depth and breadth of its faculty, with fields of interests that include comparative and historical sociology, demography, race relations, social change in advanced and underdeveloped countries, social movements, sociology of culture, sociology of law, sex roles and sociology of religion. *Undergraduate Course Highlights: Social Movements and Political Action; Race/Ethnic Relations: International Comparisons; Feminist Theory.*

The special character of Berkeley's graduate program is its emphasis on individual interests, combined with rigorous training in theory and method. Rejecting orthodoxy, the department's structure and culture support students who pursue their own intellectual concerns, stimulated and helped by the faculty and their peers. The department encourages originality, theoretical ambition, and original empirical research.

✦ Key Faculty

Michael Burawoy: Labor; methodology; capitalism.
Nancy Chodorow: Feminist theory; psychoanalytic theory; psychoanalysis and feminism; psychoanalytic sociology; family; gender.
Laura Enriquez: Development in Latin America; rural sociology; social policy; social movements; Nicaragua; Cuba.
Peter Evans: Development; comparative political economy; state and industrialism; Latin America.
Other interesting faculty: Troy Duster, Harry Edwards, Todd Gitlin, Thomas Gold, Arlie Hochschild, Michael Hout (Chair), Jerome Karabel, and Kristin Luker.
Admissions Information: (Address as above).

University of California, Santa Barbara

Sociology

Department of Sociology
University of California
Santa Barbara, CA 93106

Degrees: M.A., Ph.D.
Phone 805/893-3630
Fax 805/893-3324

The Department of Sociology at UCSB has always been on the experimental edge of the field. Faculty have achieved distinction in the fields of economy and society, feminist studies, ethnomethodology and conversation analysis, sociology of culture, social movements, networks, urban studies, religion, organizational studies, global studies, and sociology of race and ethnicity. The department has particular strength in classical theory, quantitative methods, and qualitative techniques. UCSB has a 5–6 year M.A./Ph.D. program. *Course Highlights: Education and Society; The Sociology of Development: Globalization and the Nation-State.*

✦ Key Faculty

Richard Appelbaum: Urban growth and public policy; sociology of housing; economy and society; social theory; Marxism and critical theory; global economic systems.

Kum-Kum Bhavnani: Race, gender, class, and culture; social psychology; feminist epistemology; representations theory.

Jon Cruz: Culture; mass media; race and ethnicity; social theory; popular culture.

John Foran: Development and social change; social movements; revolutions; comparative historical methods; Latin America; Middle East.

Sara Fenstermaker: Women and work; gender inequality; deviance; feminist studies.

Avery Gordon: Feminist theory; cultural studies; social theory.

Connie McNeely: Political sociology; comparative and historical sociology; development, culture, race, and ethnicity; complex organizations; quantitative and historical methods.

John Mohr: Organizational theory; sociology of culture.

Harvey Molotch: Urban growth; media studies; domination.

Beth Schneider: Sexuality; feminist studies; social movements; AIDS; political sociology; family.

Denise Segura: Gender; labor; feminist studies; Chicano studies; race relations.

University of California, Santa Cruz

Sociology

Department of Sociology
University of California
Santa Cruz, CA 95064

Degrees: B.A., Ph.D.
Graduate Phone 408/459-3168
Undergraduate Phone 408/459-4306

The undergraduate sociology major at UCSC is a flexible program. It serves as a basis of a liberal education for students interested in the study of contemporary society and problems and issues of current concern. To insure exposure to the range of the field of sociology, students are required to complete at least one course in each of the following clusters, concentrating on one cluster as their area of expertise: Institutional Analysis (political sociology, family, organizations); Social Psychology (nonverbal communication, group process, and deviance and conformity); and Inequality and Social Change (class, race and gender, Third World countries, and social movements). *Undergraduate Course Highlights: Drugs in Society; Political Consciousness; Development and Underdevelopment.*

The graduate program is a doctoral program stressing sociological theory and methods as well as independent work. Faculty members work in the following areas: political sociology, social inequality, social psychology, feminist theory and the sociology of gender, deviance, race and ethnicity, social movements, sociology of medicine, political economy and economic sociology, historical and comparative analysis, capitalism and nature, language and social interaction, development and underdevelopment in the Third World, culture and mass media, and law and crime. Social change and research concerns cluster around environmental, racial, feminist, Latin American, peace, and class issues. *Graduate Course Highlights: Sociology of the Environment; Feminist Theory; Global Development Theory; Class, Culture, and Movement.*

✦ Key Faculty

Pamela Roby: Women and work; sociology of learning; social policy; sociology of emotions; feminism; leadership and social change.
John Brown Childs: Sociology of knowledge; religion and social action; elitist and populist social movements.
Robert Connell: Social theory; global social structure; gender relations; masculinity; sexuality; education and social justice; intellectuals.
Hardy Frye: Race and ethnicity; political sociology; field methods; social movements.
Walter Goldfrank: Social change; historical sociology; world systems.
Paul Lubeck: Political sociology; political economy; newly industrializing states; sociology of development; religion and social movements.
Mark Traugott: Social movements and revolution; social theory; historical sociology.
Graduate Admissions Information: Graduate Division; University of California; Santa Cruz, CA 95064; Phone 408/459-2301.

University of Colorado at Boulder

Social Conflict

Department of Sociology
Campus Box 327
University of Colorado
Boulder, Colorado 80309

Degrees: B.A., M.A., Ph.D.

Phone   303/492-7080
Fax   303/492-5105

The Concentration in Social Conflict prepares students to analyze and resolve conflict. It develops their third-party-neutral skills, such as mediation, in combination with intervention skills for social transformation and justice. This preparation is done within the framework of sociological theory and method, through seminars, internships, research, mediation training, and visiting lecturers from the peacemaking professions. Trained as sociologists with expertise in conflict management, graduates are prepared for positions in survey research, opinion polling, social services administration, social impact analysis, criminal justice and conflict intervention and consultation.

The undergraduate major in sociology is offered for students of peace and conflict processes. Students must complete an introductory course and five additional courses in the concentration.

The Masters program offers a working degree for career development in conflict-related fields and for mid-career professionals. Students take 30 credit hours.

For a Ph.D. degree, a student takes at least 30 credit hours at the university, meets sociological theory, methods, and statistical proficiency requirements, meets the Social Conflict seminar and practicum requirements, passes preliminary and comprehensive exams, and prepares and defends a dissertation.

✦ *Key Faculty*

Martha Gimenez: Population theory; stratification; Marxist theory; feminist theory; creator, Progressive Sociologists Network.
Thomas Mayer: Stratification; war; revolutions; analytical Marxism.

University of Wisconsin   Sociology & Rural Sociology

University of Wisconsin
Departments of Sociology and
    Rural Sociology
1180 Observatory Drive
Madison, WI 53706

Degrees: M.A., Ph.D.

Phone   608/262-4863
Fax   608/265-5389

To complete a Masters degree, students must complete 24 credits and a thesis. The course work includes requirements in statistics, methods, and theory. Upon completion of the requirements, M.A. candidates take a two-hour oral exam.

Ph.D. students study advanced statistics, methods, and theory as well as graduate seminars in sociology. The student must also complete a minor in an area outside Sociology and Rural Sociology.

A progressive research center, the Havens Center for the Study of Social Structure and Social Change is associated with the Sociology

Department. It organizes an extensive program of extended visits of radical scholars from around the world who conduct lectures and seminars throughout the year. *Course Highlights: Grassroots Development in the Third World; Rural Population Trends and Problems.*

✦ Key Faculty

Stephen Bunker: Ecology; political economy; Third World.

Jane Collins: Environmental impacts of agricultural practices; women; environment; theoretical approaches to unwaged labor.

Joseph Elder: Relationship between ethnic conflicts and economic change; role of religion in contemporary political movements; resolution of conflict; South Asia.

Jack Kloppenberg, Jr.: Local indigenous knowledge; access to and control over genetic resources; genetic erosion; species extinction.

Russell Middleton: Grassroots approaches to development in the Third World; Southeast Asia.

Dennis O'Hearn: Comparative political economy of development; resource extraction economies.

Ann Orloff: Gender and politics; social policy; state theory; state building; comparative and historical research methods.

Albert Palloni: Health; fertility; mortality; Latin America.

Joel Rogers: Labor relations; theory of democratic governance; radical social theory.

Gay Seidman: Third World labor movements; South Africa; Brazil.

Cynthia Truelove: Rural industrialization and women; development; Latin America.

Erik Olin Wright: Political economy; Marxism, advanced capitalist societies; theories of the state.

Urban Planning

Cornell University

Urban & Regional Planning

Cornell University
City and Regional Planning
W. Sibley Hall
Ithaca, NY 14853-6701

Degrees: M.A., Ph.D.

Phone	607/255-6848
Fax	607/255-6681

The department offers the opportunity to focus on domestic and international issues of development and planning. It also houses university-wide programs on African Development, International Studies in Planning, and International Development and Women. *Course Highlights: Political Economy of Gender and Work; Regional Planning and Development in Developing Nations; Legal Aspects of International Planning.*

✦ Key Faculty

Lourdes Benería: Labor economics; women's work; international economics; economic development; Latin America; Europe.

Susan Christopherson: Changing industrial structures and regional development; gender issues in planning; social geography; culture of cities.

Pierre Clavel: Graduate Faculty Representative; administration; politics; local economic development.

John Forester: Planning organization; planning theory; critical social theory; health planning; evaluation and policy analysis.

William Goldsmith: United States urban policy; political economy; international urbanization; development and underdevelopment; Latin American studies; Latin America; Caribbean.

Porus Olpadwala: Political economy; comparative international development; international rural development; technology development and transfer; transnational corporations; Asia; Western Europe.

Admissions Information: Admissions; 110-114 Sage Graduate Center; Cornell University; Ithaca, NY 14853; Phone 607/255-4884.

Massachusetts Institute of Technology

Urban Studies & Planning

Massachusetts Institute of Technology
Department of Urban Studies and Planning
77 Massachusetts Avenue, 7-338
Cambridge, MA 02139

Degrees: M.C.P., Ph.D.

Phone	617/253-3270
Fax	617/253-7402

The Department of Urban Studies and Planning offers a Master's degree in City Planning with the option to specialize in developing countries and regional planning. The Ph.D. program focuses on training individuals for research and teaching in the areas of applied social research and planning. *Course Highlights: Planning Roles and Institutions in Developing Countries; International Environmental Negotiation; Housing and Urban Policy.*

✦ *Key Faculty*

Phil Clay: National urban policy; low-income housing; community-based development organizations.
Lawrence Susskind: Environmental management; dispute resolution; facility siting; impact assessment; land use and growth management; intergovernmental relations; public participation in local decision making.
Admissions Information: Admissions Coordinator; (Address as above); Phone 617/253-1907.

Tufts University

Tufts University
Department of Urban and
    Environmental Policy
97 Talbot Avenue
Medford, MA 02155

Urban & Regional Planning

Degree: M.A. in Public Policy

Phone 617/627-3394
Fax   617/627-3377

The curriculum is centered on two spheres of interest: urban social policy and environmental policy. Topics in urban social policy include poverty, affordable housing, community economic development, child and family policy, and nonprofit management. Topics in environmental policy include natural resource conservation and management, sustainable development, environmental protection, risk communication, and social management of technology. The program's distinctive features include an interdisciplinary approach; a focus on field-based education; an emphasis on values, democratic principles, and citizen initiatives in setting a public agenda; an appreciation of the centrality of nonprofit organizations in implementing programs; and a concern for the local and distributive impacts of public policy. *Urban Policy Course Highlights: National Urban Policy; Gender in Public Policy; Seminar on Government and the Family. Environmental Policy Course Highlights: Environmental Policy Analysis; Topics in Ecology and Resource Management; Environmental Economics.*

+ Key Faculty

Rachel Bratt: Housing and community development; needs of low-income households; role of community-based housing organizations.
Ann Helwege: Stabilization programs; poverty in Latin America; international economic development; environmental economics.
Robert Hollister: Leadership and management of nonprofit organizations.
Francine Jacobs: Human service program evaluation; early intervention; family support; child care; policies for children with handicaps or chronic illness.
Sheldon Krimsky: Role of science in public policy; social theories of risk and biotechnology.
Molly Mead: Nonprofit management; organizational development; issues affecting women and/or gay communities and training; education methodologies.
Admissions Information: Tufts University; Graduate School; 210 Packard Avenue; Medford, MA 02155; Phone 617/627-3395.

University of California, Berkeley

College of Environmental Design
Department of City and Regional Planning
University of California
Berkeley, CA 94720-1850

Urban & Regional Planning

Degrees: M.C.P., Ph.D.

Phone 510/642-3257
Fax 510/642-1641

The Department of City and Regional Planning focuses on the discipline of urban planning and on the operation of planning ideas in the urban and regional fields. The Master of City Planning degree offers an opportunity to specialize in one of seven concentration areas: land use planning, housing and project development, regional development and planning, urban design, community development/services, transportation planning, and environmental planning and policy. In addition, students interested in international studies can supplement these concentrations with a departmental minor in international and comparative studies. Programs of study for the Ph.D. stress preparation in research methods, spatial and regional analysis, methods of the policy sciences, development theory, historical processes, the guidance of change, and the critical appraisal of alternative courses of change. *Course Highlights: Studies in Regional Growth and Development; Third World Urban Development Issues and Policy Options; Community Development: Theory and Practice.*

+ *Key Faculty*

Manuel Castells: Urban sociology; planning for developing countries; technological change.
David Dowall: Urban economics; land use planning.
Admissions Information: Graduate Admissions Assistant; (Address as above); Phone 510/643-9440; Fax 510/642-1641.

University of California, Los Angeles

Regional & Urban Planning

Urban Planning Department
405 Hilgard Avenue
University of California
Los Angeles, CA 90024-1467

Degrees: M.A., Ph.D.

Phone   310/825-8957
Fax   310/206-5566

Recently established as a separate department within a new School of Public Policy and Social Research, the Department of Urban Planning offers several fields of specialization: the built environment and physical planning, social and community planning, regional and international development, and environment planning and policy. The department is committed to interdisciplinary study and is flexible to adapt requirements to student interests and needs. *Course Highlights: Urbanization and Rural Development in Third World Countries; Homelessness: Housing and Social Service Issues; Race, Gender, Culture, and Cities.*

+ *Key Faculty*

Susanna Hecht: Resource-based development; international development studies; tropical development; popular resistance movements.
Admissions Information: (Address as above); Phone 310/825-0525.

University of Illinois at Urbana-Champaign

Urban & Regional Planning

University of Illinois at Urbana-Champaign
Department of Urban and Regional Planning
907½ West Nevada Street
Urbana, IL 61801

Degrees: B.A.U.P., M.U.P., Ph.D.

Phone   217/333-3890
Fax   217/244-1717

The Department of Urban and Regional Planning at the University of Illinois at Urbana-Champaign conducts research activities across the scope of planning issues, including housing, community and economic development, land use and transportation modeling, historical interpretation, land use and water quality, and information and decision support systems. Degrees offered are the Bachelor of Arts in Urban Planning, the Master of Urban Planning, and the Doctor of Philosophy in Regional Planning. *Course Highlights: Ecological Systems in Planning; Urban Social Problems and Planning; Public Involvement in Resource Management and Environmental Planning.*

✦ Key Faculty

Kenneth Reardon: Community development; neighborhood planning theory; organizational behavior.
Graduate Admissions Information: Masters Program Director or Ph.D. Program Advisor; (Address as above); Phone 217/333-3890.
Undergraduate Admissions Information: Office of Admissions and Records; University of Illinois at Urbana-Champaign; 10 Administration Bldg.; 506 South Wright Street; Urbana, IL 61801; Phone 217/333-0302.

OTHER PROGRAMS

Cleveland State University
Urban Planning, Design, and Development
Maxine Goodman Levin College of Urban Affairs
1737 Euclid Avenue
Cleveland, OH 44115

Degrees: M.U.P.D.D., M.P.A., M.S.U.S., Ph.D.
Phone 216/687-2136
Fax 216/687-9239

✦ Key Faculty: Norman Krumholz, Dennis Keating

Morgan State University
City and Regional Planning Program
Jenkins 334
Baltimore, MD 21239

Degree: M.C.R.P.
Phone 410/319-3208
Fax 410/319-3786

Pratt Institute
Graduate Center for Planning and the
    Environment
200 Willoughby Avenue
Brooklyn, NY 11205

Degree: M.S.C.R.P.
Phone 718/636-3414
Fax 718/636-3432

✦ Key Faculty: Ronald Shiffman
Grad. Faculty Contact: Ron Shiffman, Phone 718/636-3414

University of Minnesota
Humphrey Institute of Public Affairs
301—19th Avenue South
Minneapolis, MN 55455

Degree: M.P.
Phone   612/625-9505
Fax   612/625-6351

Women's Studies

Cornell University

Gender and Global Change
Cornell University
33 Warren Hall
209 Triphammer Road
Ithaca, NY 14850

Gender & Global Change

Degree: M.A. (participating departments)

Phone   607/255-1680
Fax   607/255-0784

The interdisciplinary program on Gender and Global Change focuses on comparative historical analyses of changing patterns of gender relations within the broad framework of feminist scholarship and analyses of global change. The program seeks to deepen our understanding of how gender intersects with other dimensions of identity, how different experiences of gender shape social and economic change, and how gender relationships and identities themselves are reproduced and transformed in different parts of the world. The program encourages dialogue and collaboration among scholars, policymakers, political activists and others working toward understanding patterns of gender dynamics and changing structural and cultural practices. GGC is not a degree granting program, as students who work on topics related to gender and global change must fulfill their degree requirements in one of the fields of the graduate school or one of the professional schools. However, the program provides a base from which students can develop an interdisciplinary program of study drawing upon the abundant resources of Cornell University. The only course offered by the program is *Global Perspectives on Gender*.

✦ Key Faculty

Josephine Allen: Human service studies.
N'Dri Assié-Lumumba: Education; Africana/Women's studies.
Lourdes Benería: Labor economics; women's work; international economics; economic development; Latin America; Europe.
Shelley Feldman: Social restructuring and the transformation of work in the U.S. and South Asia; household food production systems; analyses of agricultural sustainability in the upland regions of Southeast Asia.
Billy Jean Isbell: Anthropology; Latin America.
Kathryn March: Anthropology; South Asia.
Leslie Pierce: Near East Studies.
Mary Rolban: History; Latin America.
Admissions Information: (Address as above).

Eastern Michigan University   Women's Studies

Women's Studies Program
720 Pray-Harrold
Eastern Michigan University
Ypsilanti, MI 48197

Degrees: Undergrad Minor, M.L.S.

Phone   313/487-1177
Fax   313/485-9592

A minor in Women's Studies requires 21 semester hours of classes from the department, which aims to provide intellectual perspective and life-enriching skills to both women and men. Insights into the psychology of women, the impact of women on social structures, and the changes women make are examples of some of the issues examined within this minor. *Course Highlights: Anthropology of Women; Sexism and Education; Women in Literature.*

The Master's of Liberal Studies (M.L.S.) is an interdisciplinary program divided into three sections: a primary concentration in Women's Studies; a complementary concentration; and a capstone experience. Students are required to take several courses from two additional departments besides women's studies. Courses are offered in a variety of areas including history, psychology, sociology, physical education, educational leadership, educational psychology, and human, environmental, and consumer resources. *Course Highlights: Technology, Social Change, and the Role of Women; Feminist Thought; Achievement and Gender.*

✦ *Key Faculty*

Christina Jose-Kampsmer: Founder, Women and Prison Program, which facilitates children's visits with their mothers in prison.
Admissions Information: Office of Admissions; 401 Pierce Hall; Eastern Michigan University; Ypsilanti, MI 48197; Phone 313/487-3060.

Emory University   Women's Studies

Program in Women's Studies
210 Physics Building
Emory University
Atlanta, GA 30322

Degree: Ph.D.

Phone   404/727-0096
Fax   404/727-4659

Within this interdisciplinary Ph.D. program, students may focus on a variety of topics pertaining to the study of women, gender, and feminist theory. Courses are offered in conjunction with departments in the humanities and social sciences, as well as African Studies, Latin American Studies, Educational Studies, and the Candler School of Theology. *Course Highlights: Literature, Politics and the Woman Writer; Feminist Theory; Women's Studies Colloquium.*

✦ *Key Faculty*

Martine Watson Brownley: Director, Women's Studies; Professor of English; eighteenth-century literature; women's studies.

Admissions Information: Dean; Graduate School of Arts and Sciences; 202 Administration Building; Emory University; Atlanta, GA 30322.

George Washington University

George Washington University
Women's Studies Program
Funger 217
2201 G Street, NW
Washington, DC 20052

Women's Studies

Degree: M.A.

Phone   202/994-6942

Two programs in Women's Studies at George Washington University are concerned with improving the status of women: the M.A. in public policy with a concentration in Women's Studies, and the M.A. in Women's Studies. Both programs share an initial curriculum in feminist theory and feminist research methods. For the public policy course of study, students continue with a more traditional public policy curriculum. The M.A. in Women's Studies is interdisciplinary. Students focus on one liberal arts discipline in addition to women's studies. *Course Highlights: Historical Feminism; Women and the Law; Women and Violence.*

✦ *Key Faculty*

Cynthia Deitch: Internship placement; feminist methodology; comparison of men's and women's living standards; international division of labor.

Phyllis Palmer: Housework from a feminist perspective; racial differences among women; public policy and its role in legitimizing sex, race, and class.

Barbara Miller: Infanticide in India; discrimination against females in India.

Admissions Information: Office of Graduate Admissions; The George Washington University; Washington, DC 20052.

Mankato State University   Women's Studies

Women's Studies Dept. Chair
Mankato State University
PO Box 8400 MSU 64
Mankato, MN 56002-8400

Degrees: B.A., B.S., M.S.

Phone   507/389-2077
Fax   507/389-6377

The Women's Studies Department offers both a B.A. and B.S. as well as a minor in the field. The B.A. emphasizes a liberal arts approach, providing a general academic background about women, their contributions and histories, and their relationships to other women, men, institutions, and culture. The B.S. degree focuses on specific substantive skills and a career orientation as well as an academic knowledge base. This degree requires an internship and an integrative paper. *Course Highlights: Women, Poverty, and Welfare Systems of Oppression; Women in Art; Family Violence.*

The Masters of Science program is interdisciplinary, allowing the student to develop her or his own program drawing from the humanities and social sciences. The aim of the program is to train activists and leaders who wish to promote social change in a variety of settings. Grassroots activism is especially encouraged. *Course Highlights: Women and Spirituality; Women and Aging; Women of Color.*

✦ Key Faculty

Donna Langston: Feminist theory; international feminism; race/class intersections.
Carol Perkins: Feminist education; intersection of race, class, and gender on women's educational histories; film criticism.
Gina Scuteri Rosabal: Intersections of sexism, racism, homophobia, classism, and other systems of oppression; feminist jurisprudence; Lesbian issues; Latina and Chicana women.
Admissions Information: (Address as above).

New School for Social Research   Gender Studies & Feminist Theory

New School for Social Research
Gender Studies and Feminist Theory
65 Fifth Avenue
New York, NY 10003

Degree: M.A.
Phone   212/229-5870 or
              800/523-5411
Fax   212/229-5315

Gender Studies looks at both men and women and studies the differences central to all social relations. Feminist theory studies the organization of power arrangements between the sexes. In analyzing and interpreting a wide range of social and cultural practices and politics through the lens of gender, one encounters other forms of power differences. Therefore, the M.A. degree provides critical, historical, and theoretical approaches to the study of gender. The program consists of twelve courses as well as an individual research project designed and executed by each student. *Course Highlights: Black Feminist Theory; Gender Entrapment; Beyond Domination.*

✦ *Key Faculty*

Ann Snitow: Feminist theory; cultural studies.
Jacqueline Alexander: Feminism; sexuality and the state in the Caribbean.
Admissions Information: Graduate Faculty Admissions; New School for Social Research; 65 Fifth Avenue, Room 110; New York, NY 10003; Phone 800/523-5411.

Sarah Lawrence College   Women's History

Women's History   Degree: M.A.
Sarah Lawrence College
1 Mead Way
Bronxville, NY 10708-5999   Phone   914/395-2405

The program introduces students to the growing historical literature on women, to feminist theory in relation to women's history, and to research methods and resources in the field. Students also intensively study a variety of related topical areas that consider the impact of gender, social class, race, ethnicity, and sexual orientation on women's experience in culture and society. While concentrating their efforts on historical issues, students may also pursue related topics in women's studies across the curriculum. *Course Highlights: Feminist Theory and Women's History; The Literature of Women's History.*

✦ *Key Faculty*

Elisabeth Israels Perry: Director, Women's History Department; U.S. women; politics; reform, especially in New York.
Admissions Information: Director; Graduate Studies Program; Sarah Lawrence College; 1 Mead Way; Bronxville, NY 10708-5999.

State University of New York, Albany

Women's Studies

State University of New York at Albany
Women's Studies Department
Social Sciences Bldg., Room 341
University at Albany
1400 Washington Avenue
Albany, NY 12222

Degrees: Undergrad Minor, B.A., concentration on M.A.

Phone   518/442-4220
Fax   518/442-4936

The curriculum explores how institutionalized sexism, racism, classism, and heterosexism limit human achievement and dignity, and examines the changes necessary for society to eliminate these limitations. The department's strengths stretch across disciplines, including biology, and interdisciplinary areas such as lesbian and gay studies, Latin American-Caribbean Studies, and global perspectives, particularly Africa, Latin America, and Asia. Internship with a feminist mentor, linked to a seminar, is required for undergraduate majors. There are also opportunities to work with the Center for Women and Government and to pursue legislative internships. *Course Highlights: Gender and Class in Latin American Development; Diversity and Visual Art; Black Women in U.S. History.*

✦ *Key Faculty*

Vivien Ng: Chinese history; sexuality.
Linda Nicholson: Feminist theory; graduate study.
Lillian Williams: Black women's history.
Linda Pershing: Folklore; anthropology; undergraduate study.
Bonnie Spanier: Science and sexuality.
Francine Frank: Linguistics; Hispanic studies.

OTHER PROGRAMS

Feminist Studies
Goddard College
Plainfield, VT 05667

Degree: B.A.
Phone   802/454-8311
Fax   802/454-8017

SCHOOLS

American University, DC, 7, 25, 31

Antioch University, Yellow Springs, OH, 73

Arizona, University of, Tucson, 51

Binghamton University, Binghamton, NY, 97

Boston College, Chestnut Hill, MA, 97

Boston University, MA, 87

Brandeis University, Waltham, MA, 74

California State University, Los Angeles, 49

California, University of, Berkeley, 2, 5, .10-12, 20, 33, 39, 46-47, 52, 58, 64, 66, 80-81, 94-95, 101, 109

California, University of, Davis, 11, 56

California, University of, Los Angeles, 15, 53-54, 59, 110

California, University of, Riverside, 33

California, University of, San Francisco, 11

California, University of, Santa Barbara, 12, 102

California, University of, Santa Cruz, 3, 40-41, 47-48, 55, 103-104

Centro de Ecologia y Desarrollo, Mexico, 30

City University of New York, 13, 17, 67

Clark University, Worcester, MA, 17, 26, 57

Cleveland State University, OH, 111

Colorado, University of, Boulder, 81

Columbia University, NY, 7-8, 30, 43, 63, 89-90

Cornell University, NY, 1, 17, 24, 27, 49, 74, 90, 98, 107, 113

Denver, University of, CO, 30, 41, 43, 82

Earlham School of Religion, Richmond, IN, 75

Eastern Michigan University, Ypsilanti, 114

Emory University, Atlanta, GA, 114-115

Evergreen State College, WA, 45

Five College Program, Amherst, MA, 75

Franklin and Marshall College, PA, 32

Friends World Program, Southampton, NY, 45

George Mason University, Fairfax, VA, 76-77

George Washington University, Washington, DC, 115

Georgia, University of, Athens, 18

Goddard College, Plainfield, VT, 118

Guilford College, Greensboro, NC, 39

Hampshire College, MA, 1-2, 75

Harvard University, MA, 30, 37, 67, 99

Howard University, DC, 15

Illinois, University of, Champaign-Urbana, 18, 110-111

Institute of Development Studies, UK, 27

Institute of Social Studies, The Netherlands, 30

Johns Hopkins University, Baltimore, MD, 91, 100

Juniata College, Huntingdon, PA, 77-78

Kentucky, University of, Lexington,13

Loma Linda University, Loma Linda, CA, 92-93

London, University of, 19-20, 65

Long Island University, NY, 45

Maine, University of, Orono, 3

Manchester College, North Manchester, IN, 78

Manhattan College, Bronx, NY, 78

Mankato State University, Mankato, MN, 116

Massachusetts Institute of Technology, Cambridge, 107

Massachusetts, University of, Amherst, 21, 34, 76

Michigan State University, East Lansing, 17

Michigan, University of, Ann Arbor, 4

Mills College, Oakland, CA, 43

Minnesota, University of, Minneapolis, 112

Minnesota, University of, St. Paul, 5

Morgan State University, Baltimore, MD, 111

New College of California, San Francisco, 68

New School for Social Research, NY, 8, 32-33, 87, 101, 116-117

New York University, New York, 69

North Carolina, University of, Chapel Hill, 18

North Dakota, University of, Grand Forks, 83

Northeastern University, Boston, MA, 69

Northern Arizona University, Flagstaff, 17

Notre Dame, University of, IN, 35-36, 83, 88

Ohio State University, Columbus, 50

Pratt Institute, Brooklyn, NY, 111

Princeton University, NJ, 63

Rutgers University, NJ, 17, 57, 93

San Francisco State University, CA, 8, 28, 51, 64

San Francisco, University of, CA, 42, 84

Sarah Lawrence College, Bronxville, NY, 117

Southern Maine, University of, Portland, 36

St. Thomas, University of, St. Paul, 85

Stanford University, CA, 9-10, 19-20, 70

State University of New York, Albany, 118

State University of New York, Buffalo, 66

Syracuse University, Syracuse, NY, 79

Texas, University of, Austin, 22

Tufts University, Medford, MA, 80, 108-109

Tulane University, New Orleans, LA, 95

Utah, University of, Salt Lake City, 37

Washington, University of, Seattle, 60

Whittier Law School, Los Angeles, CA, 70

Wisconsin, University of, Madison, 28, 56, 105

Yale University, New Haven, CT, 71

COURSES

A

Achievement and Gender, 114
Advanced Insect Ecology, 48
Advanced Readings in Political Economy and
  Sustainability, 48
African Autobiography, 16
African Crisis, 25-26
African Cultural Formation and Identity, 15
African Ecology and Development, 59
African Peoples in the World System, 7
African Protest Movements, 50
African Women's History, 16
Afro-American Sociolinguistics: Black English, 53
Aging and Aging Policy in the 1990s, 99
Agrarian Origins of Underdevelopment in Latin
  America, 19
Agricultural Ecology, 4
Agriculture Ecology, 2, 48
Agriculture in Development, 93
Agriculture in Third World Economies, 57
Agroecology and Sustainable Agriculture, 3, 48
AIDS and the Law, 67
Alcohol and Drug Dependency, 93
American Indian Tribal Governments, 99
American Sixties, 80
Anatomy of Peace, 79
Anthropological Approaches to Study of Buddhism
  in Asia, 24
Anthropology of Development, 12, 25
Anthropology of Mass Media and Popular Culture,
  12
Anthropology of Women, 114
Anthropology of World System, 12
Asian Americans and Public Policy, 55

B

Beyond Domination, 117
Biological Control of Pests, 2
Black American Family, 50
Black Autobiography, 56
Black Feminist Theory, 117
Black Role Models, 50
Black Women in U.S. History, 118
Blacks, Film, and Society, 56
Brazilian Politics, 87

C

Chicano History, 49, 53

Chicano Literature, 49
Chicano Psychological Issues, 49
Children's Rights Seminar, 71
Chinese Immigration, 54
Circumpolar Peoples, 10
Civilization of South Asia, 78
Class, Culture, and Movement, 104
Collective Action, 81-82
Community Development: Theory and Practice, 109
Community Nutrition, 90, 94
Community Programs Laboratory, 93
Community, Identity, and Nationalism, 84
Comparative Gender Systems, 10
Comparative Politics of the Middle East, 87
Comparative Slavery Systems, 53
Conflict Resolution: Theory and Practice, 81
Contemporary Issues in Urban Poverty Research, 59
Contemporary Spanish-American Drama, 22
Critical and Theoretical Perspectives in Black
  Women's Writings, 56
Critical Issues in U.S.-Asian Relations, 55
Crosscultural Encounters, 84
Crosscultural Literacy, 42
Cultural and Human Ecology, 59
Cultural Construction of Gender, 7
Cultural Foundations of Education, 41
Cultural History of Vietnam, 24
Cultural World Views of Native America, 54
Culture and Environment, 59, 61
Culture and Political Economy, 8
Culture and Power (Mesoamerica and Beyond), 9
Culture and the Individual, 12
Culture, Media, and Los Angeles, 53

D

Decolonization of South Asia, 63
Development and Underdevelopment, 55, 58, 97,
  103-104, 107
Diversity and Visual Art, 118
Domestic Relations, 68
Drugs in Society, 103
Dynamic Systems in Population and Community
  Ecology, 4
Dynamics of Indian Societies, 52
Dynamics of Neotropical Rainforests, 4

E

Early Childhood Education, 39
East Asia Education, 39
Ecodevelopment, 48
Ecological Systems in Planning, 111

Ecology and Economy of Third World Societies, 26
Ecology and the Environment, 1
Ecology of Agricultural Systems, 1
Ecology of Agriculture, 5
Ecology of Agroecosystems, 4
Econometrics Colloquia, 34
Economic Demographics, 33
Economic Development, 13, 31-34, 36-37, 40, 59, 98, 107-109, 111, 113
Economic Development and Education in the Third World, 40
Economic Development and Planning, 33
Economic Development of the Middle East, 37
Economic Development Policy, 31
Economic Expansion, Social Change, and Class Formation in the Periphery, 97
Economic Geography and Development Theory, 59
Economic System of the Soviet Union, 36
Economic Theory Colloquia, 34
Economics of Gender and Discrimination, 36
Economics of World Regions, 31
Ecosystem Ecology, 46
Education and Society, 102
Education of Black Americans, 56
Employment Discrimination, 69
Environment and Development, 37
Environment and Society, 99
Environmental Economics, 21, 31, 33, 35, 37, 108-109
Environmental Ideas, 79
Environmental Issues in Latin America, 45
Environmental Law and Processes, 70
Environmental Law and Regulation, 46-47
Environmental Nutrition, 90
Environmental Philosophy and Ethics, 45-46
Environmental Policy Analysis, 108
Epidemiology of Nutrition, 91
Ethical Issues in Public Health, 92
Ethics and Development, 82
Ethics of Development, 84
Ethnic and Cultural Diversity in Health Status and Behavior, 94
Ethnic and Cultural Factors in Conflict, 76
Ethnic Community Practicum, 51
Evaluation in the Schools, 40

F
Family Violence, 116
Federal Civil Rights Litigation, 68
Feminist Theory, 8-9, 34, 83, 101-105, 115-118

Feminist Theory and Women's History, 117
Feminist Thought, 114
Field Entomology, 2
Field Study and Cross Cultural Education, 39
Filipino-American Community Issues, 55
Film and Social Change, 16
Folk Music of South Asia, 54
Food and Culture, 7
Food and Nutrition: A Public Health Perspective, 90
Food and Society, 7
Food Dilemmas of Latin America, 22
Food Security in Africa: Policy, Planning, and Interventions, 27
Food, Agriculture, and Society, 1
Foreign Assistance and Economic Development, 31
Forest and Wildland Resource Conservation, 46-47
Forest Ecology, 47

G
Gender and Class in Latin American Development, 118
Gender and Conflict, 77
Gender and Culture in Middle Eastern and Islamic Societies, 99
Gender and Development in the Americas, 100
Gender Entrapment, 117
Gender in Public Policy, 108
Gender Resources and Development, 57
Gender, Identity, and Self, 11
Gender, Law, and Public Policy, 70
Geography of Cities, 60
Geography of Inequality, 60
Global Development Theory, 104
Global Environmental Health, 93
Global Patterns of International Migration, 99
Global Peace Movements in the Information Age, 73
Global Perspectives on Gender, 113
Government and Politics in Sub-Saharan Africa, 16
Grassroots Development in the Third World, 106
Gross Human Rights Violations, 84

H
Hausa, 16
Health and Social Policy in Mexico and Latin America, 94
Health Law, 69
Hispanicamerican Film, 22
Historical Feminism, 115
History and Politics of Racism and Segregation, 49
History of Black Nationalism: A Comparative Perspective, 16

History of Economic Thought, 32-34, 36
History of U.S. People of Color, 51
HIV/AIDS: Implications for Public Health, 93
Homelessness: Housing and Social Service Issues, 110
Hopi Language and Culture, 52
Housing and Urban Policy, 108
Human and Machine Learning, 40
Human Rights and American Foreign Policy, 82
Human Rights and Global Change, 85
Human Rights and International Law, 68
Human Rights in the Third World, 69
Human Rights, 81
Humanitarian Principles and Armed Conflict, 69

I

Idea of War, 77
Ideological, Cultural, and Economic Context of Human Rights, 101
Images and Power, 98
Immigrants and Education, 41
Immigration and Ethnicity, 100
Immigration Law, 68, 70
Immigration Law and Policy, 70
Indian and Peasant Politics, 19
Indian Law, 51, 54
Inequality and Social Identity, 74
Insect-Pest Management, 5
Integrated Community Development, 93
Integrated Pest Management, 3, 5
Intercultural and Gender Issues in Conflict Resolution, 73
International Environment and Politics, 25
International Environmental Negotiation, 108
International Humanitarian Issues, 88
International Law and Organization, 78
International Nutrition: Problems, Policies, and Programs, 91
International Relations of Latin America, 88
Introduction to Economics, 19

J

Juvenile Justice, 71

L

La Nueva Cancion Latinoamericana, 55
Labor and Employment Law, 68
Labor Economics, 31-35, 107, 113
Labor in the World System, 100
Labor Movements in the Third World, 87
Land and Labor in Latin America, 8

Landscapes of the Middle East, 57
Language and Literature of Political Violence, 75
Latin American Communities, 7
Latin American History, 64
Latin American International Relations, 22
Latin American Land and Peasants, 55
Latin American Music, 22
Law and Society, 98
Legal and Illegal Violence Against Women, 98
Legal Aspects of International Planning, 107
Legislative Process, 87
Liberation Theology, 75
Life in Rural South Asia, 7
Literature of the Developing World, 79
Literature of Women's History, 117
Literature, Politics, and the Woman Writer, 115
Local Action/Global Change, 26
Local and Regional Transformation, 58-59

M

Magic of the State, 7
Magic, Religion, and Witchcraft, 12
Major Racial Minorities in the United States, 52
Managing Ethnic Conflict, 74
Mayan Languages, 22
Media Criticism, 79
Mesoamerica (Maya Text and Image), 10
Migration within and Immigration to the U.S., 64
Mind and Conflict, 77
Minorities in the Schooling Process, 40
Minority Group Politics, 54
Modern African History, 63
Modern Chinese History, 63
Modern Contemporary Jewish Thought, 64
Modern Middle East, 64
Modernity and its Discontents, 101
Moral Development, 42
Moral Thought in a Nuclear Age, 83
Multiracial Societies in Latin America, 22

N

National Defense: Military, Economic, and Cultural, 79
National Urban Policy, 108
Nationalism and Gender, 9
Nation-States, Sex, and Modernity, 97
Native American Revitalization Movements, 54
Non-Proliferation after the Cold War, 75
Nonviolence, 77, 80-81, 85
Nonviolent Social Change, 83-84
North-South Global Divide, 75

Nutrition and Behavior, 89
Nutrition Introduction in Communities: A Global Perspective, 91
Nutritional Aspects of Disease, 94
Nutritional Ecology, 89
Nutrition: A Biochemical and Physiological Basis, 94

O
Oceanic Islands, 57
Outbreak of War, 82

P
Peace, Justice, and Ethical Issues in Conflict Resolution, 73
Peasant Revolution and Village in Modern China, 76
Peasants and Industrialization, 12
People of the Andes Today, 22
Peoples and Cultures of Africa, 16
People, Land, and Food: Comparative Study of Agriculture Systems, 61
People, Poverty, and Environment in Central America, 12
Perspectives on Gender in Spanish-American Literature, 19
Perspectives on Sustainable Development in Latin America, 19
Pesticide Alternatives, 2
Pesticides and the Environment, 4
Pest-Plant Interactions, 4
Physical Anthropology, 8-9, 12
Planning Roles and Institutions in Developing Countries, 108
Political Change in the Third World, 55
Political Consciousness, 103
Political Development and Modernization, 22
Political Ecology, 9, 20, 58-59
Political Economy and Historical Geography of Latin American Development, 58
Political Economy of African Crisis, 25
Political Economy of Development Colloquia, 34
Political Economy of Gender, 32
Political Economy of Gender and Work, 107
Political Economy of Race, 53
Political Economy of Sustainable Agriculture in Latin America, 3, 48
Political Economy of the Environment, 32, 34
Political Economy of Women, 34, 37
Political, Economic, and Ecological Processes, 45
Politics and the Media, 87
Politics of American Justice, 85
Politics of Tropical and Southern Africa, 88

Population and Evolutionary Ecology, 1
Population and Poverty in the Third World, 74
Population Geography, 59
Poverty and Income Maintenance, 37
Poverty and the American Underclass, 99
Poverty Law in the U.S.: Legal Strategies for the 1990s, 67
Principles of Environmental Health, 93
Problematics in International Relations, 63
Problems in Cultural Anthropology, 9
Problems in Political Economy, 36
Problems in Urban Anthropology, 11
Prospects for Peace in the 21st Century: Alternative Futures, 73
Public Health Aspects of Maternal and Child Nutrition, 94
Public Involvement in Resource Management and Environmental Planning, 111
Public Policy and Development in Africa, 15

R
Race and Politics in the U.S., 1820-1900, 63
Race and Public Policy, 52
Race, Gender, Class, and Sexuality, 80
Race, Gender, Culture, and Cities, 110
Race/Ethnic Relations: International Comparisons, 101
Racial and Ethnic Minorities, 80
Rebellion and Revolution in the World System, 100
Refugee Health, 93
Refugees: Survival, Adaptation and Transformation, 7
Regional Cultures and Economies in the North American Past, 61
Regional Planning and Development in Developing Nations, 107
Religions and War, 78
Religious Responses to War and Violence, 75
Research Seminar on African History, 63
Rural Population Trends and Problems, 106
Rural Research and Rural Policy, 27
Rural Transformation in Postcolonial Societies, 11

S
Seminar in Alternative Labor Theories and Applied Research, 36
Seminar in Contemporary American Society, 11
Seminar on African Law, 9
Seminar on Government and the Family, 108
Seminar on the Family, 100
Seminar in Archaeological Problems, 9

Sexism and Education, 114
Sexuality and the Law, 67
Social Change in Latin America, 22
Social History of Development in Africa, 8
Social Inequality, 10, 103
Social Movements and Political Action, 101
Social Role of the Non-Conformists, 79
Social Stratification, 15, 81, 98, 100
Social Stratification in Contemporary Africa, 15
Socioeconomic Environment of Health, 92
Sociology of Development: Globalization and the Nation-State, 102
Sociology of Neighborhoods, 101
Sociology of the Environment, 104
Sociology of War, 81
Southeast Asia, 10, 21, 24, 61, 99, 106, 113
Spanish-American Short Story, 22
Spirituality for Peace and Justice, 75
Statistics for Development Policy, 27
Stigmatized Health Conditions, 11-12
Student Teaching, 42
Studies in Regional Growth and Development, 109
Survey of Nutrition: Fads and Popular Fallacies, 89
Sustainable Agriculture and Development, 45, 99
Sustainable Soil Management, 3, 48
Swahili, 16, 49
Swahili Literature, 49

T

Teaching, Learning, and Schooling in Social Context, 40-41
Technology, Social Change, and the Role of Women, 114
Theoretical Approaches to Race and Racism, 8
Theories of Social Change and Evolution, 100
Theory Development, 76-77
Third Party Roles, Resources, and Ethics, 76
Third World Health, 2, 11
Third World in the World Economy, 32
Third World Urban Development Issues and Policy Options, 109
Topics in Ecology and Resource Management, 108
Topics in the History of Sex and Gender, 63
Tropical Biology: An Ecological Approach, 4

U

Understanding Africa, 12
Understanding and Preventing Violence, 92
United States and Central America, 19
Urban Anthropology, 7, 11
Urban Economics, 36-37, 110

Urban Politics, 50, 87
Urban Social Problems and Planning, 111
Urbanization and Rural Development in Third World Countries, 110

V

Vietnamese-American Experience, 55

W

War and Coalitional Aggression, 12
War, Revolution, and Peace: Alternatives to the Adversary Process, 76
Welfare and Poverty in the 20th Century, 19
Welfare Law, 69-70
Wolof, 16
Women and Aging, 116
Women and Spirituality, 116
Women and the Law, 69, 115
Women and the U.S. Economy, 32
Women and Violence, 115
Women in Art, 116
Women in Development, 7
Women in Literature, 114
Women in the Economy, 25
Women of Africa and of the Diaspora in Liberation Movements, 49
Women of Color, 116
Women's Studies Colloquium, 115
Women, Men, and Violence, 85
Women, Poverty, and Welfare Systems of Oppression, 116
World Food Crisis, 2
World Food Patterns, 83
World Hunger and Resource Development, 60
World Politics for Precollegiate Teachers, 41

Z

Zulu, 16

FACULTY

Ablon, Joan, 12
Abrams, Barbara, 94
Akabas, Sharon, 89
Alexander, Jacqueline, 117
Allen, Josephine, 113
Altieri, Miguel, 2
Andow, David, 5
Appelbaum, Richard, 102
Arnold, Steve, 25
Assié-Lumumba, N'Dri, 113
Babcock, Barbara, 70
Balderrama, Francisco, 49
Bardhan, Pranab, 33
Barkin, David, 30
Bellow, Gary, 68
Benería, Lourdes, 107, 113
Berreman, Gerald, 10
Bertrand, Jane, 95
Bertrand, William, 95
Bhavnani, Kum-Kum, 103
Bing, Anthony, 75
Birkhoff, Juliana, 77
Blechman, Frank, 77
Blecker, Robert, 31
Block, Gladys, 95
Bourgois, Phillipe, 9
Bowles, Samuel, 35
Boyce, James, 21, 35
Bratt, Rachel, 109
Brautigam, Deborah, 25
Broad, Robin, 25
Brownley, Martine Watson, 115
Brown, Clair, 33
Brown, Ken, 78
Bruyn, Severyn, 98
Bryan, Dale, 80
Buhler, Gordon, 93
Bulmer-Thomas, Victor, 21
Bunker, Stephen, 106
Burawoy, Michael, 102
Byrnes, Ron, 39
Cagatay, Nilufer, 37
Callari, Antonio, 32
Carr, Claudia, 46
Carter, Susan, 34
Castells, Manuel, 110
Chase-Dunn, Christopher, 100

Cheru, Fantu, 25
Childs, John Brown, 104
Chodorow, Nancy, 102
Christopherson, Susan, 107
Clavel, Pierre, 107
Clay, Phil, 108
Collier, George, 9
Collier, Jane, 9
Collins, Jane, 106
Connell, Robert, 104
Contento, Isobel, 89
Cook-Huffman, Celia, 77
Crotty, James, 35
Cruz, Jon, 103
Cuellar, Jose, 51
Daar, Judith, 71
Dahlsten, Donald, 46
Davies, Susanna, 27
Davis, Natalie, 63
Deere, Carmen Diana, 21, 35
Deitch, Cynthia, 115
Demartino, George, 30
Derber, Charles, 98
Derman, William, 17
Dershowitz, Alan, 68
de Uriarte, Mercedes Lynn, 22
Dolgon, Corey, 45
Donnelly, Jack, 66
Dowall, David, 110
Downing, Peter, 41
Dunkerley, James, 19
Durham, William, 10
Duster, Troy, 102
Dutt, Amitava, 36
Dymski, Gary, 34
Eatwell, John, 32
Edelman, Marc, 13
Edgar, Bob, 15
Edmondson, Locksley, 50
Edwards, Harry, 102
Elder, Joseph, 106
Elias, Robert, 85
Enriquez, Laura, 20, 102
Epstein, Gerald, 35
Evans, Peter, 20, 102
Fahey, Joseph, 79
Fairris, David, 34
Feldman, Shelley, 99, 113
Fellman, Gordon, 74
Fenstermaker, Sara, 103

Flaherty, Diane, 35
Flaherty, Sean, 32
Floro, Maria, 31
Folbre, Nancy, 35
Foner, Eric, 63
Foran, John, 103
Ford, Richard, 26
Forester, John, 107
Fortmann, Louise, 47
Franklin, Robert, 95
Frank, Francine, 118
Frazer, Jendayi, 30
Frye, Barbara, 93
Frye, Hardy, 104
Gabriel, Teshome, 16
Gamson, William, 98
Geddes-Gonzalez, Henry, 21
Geisler, Charles, 99
Geschwender, James, 97
Gill, Gerald, 80
Gimenez, Martha, 105
Gintis, Herbert, 35
Gitlin, Todd, 102
Gliessman, Stephen, 48
Goldfischer, David, 30
Goldfrank, Walter, 104
Goldman, Robert, 66
Goldsmith, William, 107
Gold, Thomas, 102
Goodman, David, 48
Gordon, Avery, 103
Gordon, David, 32
Gordon, Edmond, 13
Grabel, Ilene, 30
Green, Jenny, 66
Green, Reginald, 27
Grendzier, Irene, 87
Griffin, Keith, 34
Gussow, Joan, 89
Haas, Jere, 91
Habicht, Jean-Pierre, 91
Hahnel, Robin, 31
Hale, Charles, 13
Hamm, Michael, 94
Hancock, Joseph, 46
Hanson, Susan, 57
Harris, Robert, 50
Hart, Richard, 93
Hecht, Susanna, 110
Heim, Carol, 35

Helwege, Ann, 109
Hesse-Biber, Sharlene, 98
Highlands, Taylor, 77
Hing, Bill, 70
Hintzen, Percy, 52
Hochschild, Arlie, 102
Hollister, Robert, 109
Hotchkiss, David, 95
Hout, Michael, 102
Howes, Candace, 36
Hunt, E.K., 37
Hurst, John, 40, 46
Isaacman, Allen, 18
Isbell, Billy Jean, 113
Ishay, Micheline, 30
Jacobs, Francine, 109
Janvry, Alain de, 5
Jarosz, Lucy, 60
Job, Jayakaran, 93
Johansen, Robert, 84
Johnson, David, 17
Jonas, Susanne, 55
Jordan, June, 52
Jose-Kampsmer, Christina, 114
Joseph, Paul, 80
Kanios, Chris, 68
Karabel, Jerome, 102
Karl, Terry, 20
Karp, David, 98
Keating, Dennis, 111
Kendall, Carl, 95
Khan, Mahmud, 95
Klare, Michael, 76
Kloppenberg, Jack Jr.,106
Kotz, David, 35
Krimsky, Sheldon, 109
Krumholz, Norman, 111
LaBoskey, Vicki, 43
Langston, Donna, 116
Latham, Michael, 91
Lawson, Victoria, 60
Leach, Melissa, 27
Leary, Virginia, 66
Lewis, Martin, 61
Lichtenstein, Gary, 43
Liebman, Matt, 4
Litwack, Leon, 64
Lopez, Gerald, 70
Lubeck, Paul, 104
Luker, Kristin, 102

Magnani, Robert, 95
Mainwaring, Scott, 88
Manor, James, 65
Manz, Beatriz, 20, 53, 59
Maran, Rita, 66
March, Kathryn, 113
Martin, Paul, 66
Martin, William G., 18
Maxwell, Simon, 27
Maybury-Lewis, David, 30
Mayer, Thomas, 82, 105
McGuinness, Hugh, 45
McMichael, Philip, 99
McNeely, Connie, 103
Mead, Molly, 109
Medley, Joseph, 37
Merchant, Carolyn, 46
Meurs, Mieke, 31
Middleton, Russell, 106
Milberg, William, 33
Miller, Barbara, 115
Miller, Raymond, 28
Mitchell, Kathryne, 60
Mitteness, Linda, 12
Mock, Nancy, 95
Modrowski, Kathleen, 46
Mohr, John, 103
Molotch, Harvey, 103
Molyneux, Maxine, 19
Morrison, Kathleen, 20
Nader, Laura, 10
Nakanishi, Don, 55
Navarro, Vicente, 92
Nelson, William, 50
Newbury, David, 18
Ng, Vivien, 118
Nicholson, Linda, 118
Nietschmann, Bernard, 59
Nissan, Elizabeth, 65
O'Hearn, Dennis, 106
Olpadwala, Porus, 107
Onate, Abdiel, 64
Ong, Aihwa, 10
Orloff, Ann, 106
Palloni, Albert, 106
Palmer, Phyllis, 115
Patton, William, 71
Perkins, Carol, 116
Perry, Elisabeth Israels, 117
Pershing, Linda, 118

Peters, Pauline, 30
Petras, James, 97
Pfohl, Stephen, 98
Philips, Peter, 37
Pierce, Leslie, 113
Pollin, Robert, 34
Pollis, Adamantia, 88
Portes, Alejandro, 100
Power, Alison, 1
Pred, Allan, 59
Quesada, James, 9
Rabinow, Paul, 10
Ralston, Richard, 56
Rao, Mohan, 35
Rapp, Rayna, 8
Reardon, Kenneth, 111
Reich, Michael, 33
Reppy, Judith, 75
Resnick, Stephen, 35
Richardson, John, 25
Richert, Anna, 43
Roby, Pamela, 104
Rogers, Joel, 106
Rolban, Mary, 113
Rosabal, Gina Scuteri, 116
Rosaldo, Reynato, 10
Rowe, Thomas, 82
Rubinstein, Robert, 79
Ruccio, David, 36
Sabry, Zak, 95
Samarasinghe, Vidyamali, 25
Sanders, Jerry, 81
Sander, Frank, 68
Saragoza, Alex, 53
Saunders, Lisa, 35
Sawers, Larry, 31
Scheper-Hughes, Nancy, 10
Schneider, Beth, 103
Schoenbrun, David, 18
Schultz, Arnold, 46
Schultz, Brian, 2
Segura, Denise, 103
Seidman, Ann, 17, 26
Seidman, Gay, 16, 106
Selden, Mark, 97
Shaikh, Anu, 33
Shiffman, Ronald, 111
Shipton, Parker, 30
Silver, Beverly, 100
Simon, William, 70

Singer, Hans, 27
Skocpol, Theda, 100
Smith, Carol, 11
Smith, Neil, 58
Snitow, Ann, 117
Sorenson, Kristin, 83
Spangler, Eve, 98
Spanier, Bonnie, 118
Stallings, Barbara, 23
Stern, Steve, 23
Stonich, Susan, 13
Strickler, Jennifer, 95
Susskind, Lawrence, 108
Takaki, Ronald, 53
Taussig, Michael, 8
Taylor, Kim, 70
Taylor, Lance, 33
Thomas-Slayter, Barbara, 26
Thompson, Carol, 17
Traugott, Mark, 104
Truelove, Cynthia, 106
Turner, James, 50
Turpin, Jennifer, 85
Turshen, Meredeth, 17
van Willigen, John, 13
Vandermeer, John, 4
Varese, Stefano, 56
Vaughan, Diane, 98
Wachtel, Howard, 31
Walker, Richard, 59
Wallerstein, Immanuel, 97
Watts, Michael, 59
Wehr, Paul, 82
Weiler, Kathleen, 80
Wilber, Charles, 36
Williams, Brett, 7
Williams, Lillian, 118
Willoughby, John, 31
Wisman, Jon, 31
Wolff, Richard, 35
Wood, David, 46
Wright, Erik Olin, 106
Zisk, Betty, 87

Food First Publications

Alternatives to the Peace Corps: A Directory of Third World and U.S. Volunteer Opportunities by Becky Buell and Annette Olson. Now in its sixth edition, this guide provides essential information on voluntary service organizations, technical service programs, work brigades, study tours, as well as alternative travel in the Third World and offers options to the Peace Corps as the principle route for people wishing to gain international experience. $6.95

BASTA! Land and the Zapatista Rebellion in Chiapas by George Collier with Elizabeth Lowery Quaratiello. The authors examine the root causes of the Zapatista uprising in southern Mexico and outline the local, national, and international forces that created a situation ripe for a violent response. $12.95

Brave New Third World? Strategies for Survival in the Global Economy by Walden Bello. Can Third World countries finish the next decade as vibrant societies? Or will they be even more firmly in the grip of underdevelopment? The outcome, Bello argues, depends on their ability to adopt a program of democratic development which would place them on equal footing in the global economy. $8.00 (Development Report)

Breakfast of Biodiversity: The Truth About Rain Forest Destruction by John Vandermeer and Ivette Perfecto. Analyzes deforestation from both an environmental and social justice perspective. Ecologists Vandermeer and Perfecto identify and untangle the "web of causality" that leads to the ravaging of rain forests, and they construct a compelling, nuanced argument that conservation alone is not enough. $16.95

Chile's Free-Market Miracle: A Second Look by Joseph Collins and John Lear. The economic policies behind the boom experienced by Chile in the 1980s under Pinochet, and continuing today, are widely touted as a model for the Third World. The authors take a closer look at the Chilean experience and uncover the downside of the model: chronic poverty and environmental devastation. $15.95

Circle of Poison: Pesticides and People in a Hungry World by David Weir and Mark Schapiro. In the best investigative style, this popular exposé documents the global scandal of corporate and government exportation of pesticides and reveals the threat to the health of consumers and workers throughout the world. $7.95

Dark Victory: The U.S., Structural Adjustment, and Global Poverty by Walden Bello, with Shea Cunningham and Bill Rau. Offers an understanding of why poverty has deepened in many countries, and analyzes the impact of Reagan-Bush economic policies: a decline of living standards in much of the Third World and the U.S. The challenge for progressives in the 1990s is to articulate a new agenda because people of the South and North suffer from the same process that preserves the interests of a global minority. $12.95

Dragons in Distress: Asia's Miracle Economies in Crisis by Walden Bello and Stephanie Rosenfeld. Economists often refer to South Korea, Taiwan, and Singapore as "miracle economies," and technocrats regard them as models for the rest of the Third World. The authors challenge these established notions and show how, after three decades of rapid growth, these economies are entering a period of crisis. The authors offer policy recommendations for structural change to break the NICs' unhealthy dependence on Japan and the U.S., and they critically examine both the positive and negative lessons of the NIC experience for the Third World. $12.95

Kerala: Radical Reform as Development in an Indian State by R.W. Franke and B.H. Chasin. Analyzes both the achievements and the limitations of the Kerala experience. In the last eighty years, the Indian state of Kerala has undergone an experiment in the use of radical reform as a development strategy that has brought it some of the Third World's highest levels of health, education, and social justice. 1994 revised edition $9.95

Needless Hunger: Voices from a Bangladesh Village by James Boyce and Betsy Hartmann. The global analysis of Food First is vividly captured here in a single village. The root causes of hunger emerge through the stories of both village landowners and peasants who live at the margin of survival. Now in its sixth printing. $6.95

No Free Lunch: Food and Revolution in Cuba Today by Medea Benjamin, Joseph Collins, and Michael Scott. Based on sources not readily available to Western researchers, this examination of Cuba's food and farming system confirms that Cuba is the only Latin American country to have eradicated hunger. $9.95

People and Power in the Pacific: The Struggle for the Post-Cold War Order by Walden Bello. Examines the extent to which events in the Asia-Pacific region reflect the so-called new world order; the future role of the U.S. and the emergence of Japan as a key economic power on the world stage. $12.00

The Philippines: Fire on the Rim by Joseph Collins. Looks at the realities following the People Power revolution in the Philippines. A choir of voices from peasants, plantation managers, clergy, farmers, prostitutes who serve U.S. military bases, mercenaries, revolutionaries and others, speak out. *Hardcover* $9.50, *Paper* $5.00

Taking Population Seriously by Frances Moore Lappé and Rachel Schurman. The authors conclude that high fertility is a response to anti-democratic power structures that leave people with little choice but to have many children. The authors do not see the solution as more repressive population control, but instead argue for education and improved standard of living. $7.95

Trading Freedom: How Free Trade Affects Our Lives, Work, and Environment edited by John Cavanagh, John Gershman, Karen Baker, and Gretchen Helmke. Contributors from Mexico, Canada, and the U.S. analyze the North American Free Trade Agreement. Drawing on the experiences of communities in Canada, the U.S., and Mexico, this comprehensive collection provides a hard-hitting critique of the current proposals for a continental free trade zone through an intensive examination of its impact on the environment, workers, consumers, and women. $5.00

Curricula

Exploding the Hunger Myths: A High School Curriculum by Sonja Williams. With an emphasis on hunger, twenty-five activities provide a variety of positive discovery experiences—role playing, simulation, interviewing, writing, drawing—to help students understand the real underlying causes of hunger and how problems they thought were inevitable can be changed. 200 pages, 8.5x11 with charts, reproducible illustrated hand-outs, resource guide and glossary. $18.00

Food First Curriculum by Laurie Rubin. Six delightfully illustrated units span a range of compelling topics including the path of food from farm to table, why people in other parts of the world do things differently, and how young people can help make changes in their communities. 146 pages, three-hole punched, 8.5x11 with worksheets and teacher's resources. $15.00

Food First Comic by Leonard Rifas. An inquisitive teenager sets out to discover the roots of hunger. Her quest is illustrated with wit and imagination by Rifas, who has based his comic on *World Hunger: Twelve Myths*. $2.00

Write or call our distributor to place book orders. All orders must be prepaid. Please add $4.00 for the first book and $1.00 for each additional book for shipping and handling.

Subterranean Company
Box 160, 265 South 5th Street
Monroe, OR 97456
(800) 274-7826

About Food First

Food First, publisher of this book, is a nonprofit research and education-for-action center. We work to identify the root causes of hunger and poverty in the United States and around the world, and to educate the public as well as policymakers about these problems.

The world has never produced so much food as it does today—more than enough to feed every child, woman, and man. Yet hunger is on the rise, with more than one billion people around the world going without enough to eat.

Food First research has demonstrated that hunger and poverty are not inevitable. Our publications reveal how scarcity and overpopulation, long believed to be the causes of hunger, are instead symptoms—symptoms of an ever-increasing concentration of control over food-producing resources in the hands of a few, depriving so many people of the power to feed themselves. In 55 countries and 20 languages, Food First materials and activism are freeing people from the grip of despair and laying the groundwork—in ideas and action—for a more democratically controlled food system that will meet the needs of all.

An Invitation to Join Us

Private contributions and membership dues form Food First's financial base. Because we are not tied to any government, corporation, or university, we can speak with strong independent voices, free of ideological formulas. The success of our programs depends not only on dedicated volunteers and staff, but on financial activists as well. All our efforts toward ending hunger are made possible by membership dues or gifts from individuals, small foundations, and religious organizations.

Each new and continuing member strengthens our effort to change a hungry world. We'd like to invite you to join in this effort. As a member you will receive a 20 percent discount on all Food First books. You will also receive our quarterly publication, Food First *News and Views*, and our timely *Backgrounders* which provide information and suggestions for action on current food and hunger crises in the United States and around the world.

All contributions to Food First are tax deductible. To join us in putting food first, just clip and return the attached coupon to

Food First/Institute for Food and Development Policy,
398 60th Street, Oakland, CA 94618
(510) 654-4400

Research internship opportunities are also available.
Call or write us for more information.

Name _____

Address _____

City/State/Zip _____

Daytime Phone ( ) _____

☐ I want to join Food First and receive a 20% discount on this and all subsequent orders. Enclosed is my tax-deductible contribution of:

☐ $100 ☐ $50 ☐ $30

PAGE	ITEM DESCRIPTION	QTY	UNIT COST	TOTAL
	T-shirts ☐ XL ☐ L ☐ M ☐ S		$12.00	

Payment Method: ☐ Check ☐ Money Order ☐ Mastercard ☐ Visa

For gift mailings, please see other side of this coupon.

Name on Card _____

Card Number _____ Exp. Date _____

Signature _____

Member discount -20%	$ _____
CA Residents 8.5%	$ _____
SUBTOTAL	$ _____
Postage/15%-UPS/20% ($2 min.)	$ _____
Membership(s)	$ _____
Contribution	$ _____
TOTAL ENCLOSED	$ _____

Make check payable to Subterranean Company, Box 160, 265 South 5th St., Monroe, OR 97456

Please send a Gift Membership to:

Name _____

Address _____

City/State/Zip _____

From _____

Please send a Gift Book to:

Name _____

Address _____

City/State/Zip _____

From _____

Please send a Resource Catalog to:

Name _____

Address _____

City/State/Zip _____

Name _____

Address _____

City/State/Zip _____

Name _____

Address _____

City/State/Zip _____

Name _____

Address _____

City/State/Zip _____